Phil Maggitti
and J. Anne Helgren

IT'S SHOW-TIME!

...and here's everything cat fanciers need to know about shows

Filled with full-color photographs
Illustrations by Tana Hakanson Monsalve

D1715263

BARRON'S

Dedication

To all cats—purebred and random bred—and the people who love them.

About the Authors

J. Anne Helgren writes the featured breed profiles for *Cats Magazine,* and has written three books on purebred cats for Barron's Educational Series. She is a professional member of the Cat Writers' Association and has written dozens of articles on cats for national and regional magazines and newspapers. Helgren has a lifetime of experience with the feline species and has conducted extensive research on cat-related topics, including interviews with breeders, judges, fanciers, and veterinarians. She lives near Sacramento, California, with her husband, Bill, one Abyssinian, and five random bred domestic cats.

Phil Maggitti, a long-time breeder and shower of Scottish Fold Cats, is a freelance writer who has published over 250 magazine articles about cats. He is well known in the cat fancy for having bred the first supreme grand champion longhaired Scottish Fold.

All inquiries should be addressed to:
Barron's Educational Series, Inc.
250 Wireless Boulevard
Hauppauge, New York 11788
http://www.barronseduc.com

International Standard Book No. 0-7641-0253-2

Library of Congress Catalog Card No. 98-20370

Library of Congress Cataloging-in-Publication Data
Helgren, J. Anne.
 It's showtime! / J. Anne Helgren, Phil Maggitti.
  p. cm.
 Includes bibliographical references and index.
 ISBN 0-7641-0253-2
 1. Cats—Showing. 2. Cats—Exhibitions. I. Maggitti, Phil.
 II. Title.
 SF445.H45 1998
 636.8'0811—dc21   98-20370
              CIP

Printed in Hong Kong

987654321

Acknowledgments

The authors would like to thank Grace Freedson, Mary Falcon, and Jan Mahood (Barron's Educational Series, Inc.), Carolyn Bussey, the Cat Fanciers' Association, The International Cat Association, American Cat Fanciers Association, American Cat Association, Cat Fanciers' Federation, American Association of Cat Enthusiasts, National Cat Fanciers' Association, the Traditional Cat Association, the Canadian Cat Association, and the United Feline Organization for all their invaluable help and advice.

Other Barron's titles by the authors:
J. Anne Helgren:
Barron's Encyclopedia of Cat Breeds 1997
Himalayan Cats: A Complete Pet Owner's Manual 1996
Abyssinian Cats: A Complete Pet Owner's Manual 1995

Phil Maggitti:
Birman Cats: A Complete Pet Owner's Manual 1996
Before You Buy That Kitten 1995
Guide to a Well-Behaved Cat 1993
Scottish Fold Cats: A Complete Pet Owner's Manual 1993

Photo Credits

Donna J. Coss: pages 3; 4; 5; 6; 14; 18; 19; 21; 22; 29 top, bottom; 31 top; 32; 33; 36; 37; 45; 47; 50; 52; 55; 58; 60; 68; 70; 77; 80; 82; 85; 88; 89; 90; 91; 92; 93; 96; 98; 99; 101; 104; 106; 112; 115; 117 top; 118; 123. Susan Green: pages 100; 107. Bob Schwartz: pages 2; 10; 11; 12; 24; 30; 31 bottom; 38; 42; 56; 62; 64; 66; 72; 75; 95; 111; 113; 117 bottom; 119.

Cover Photos

Barbara Reed: Front cover; Bob Schwartz: Back cover; Donna Coss: Inside front, inside back covers.

Contents

Chapter 1
The Show of Shows

It may be that the race is not always to the swift, nor the battle to the strong—but that's the way to bet.

—*Damon Runyon*

The first time most people visit a cat show they feel as if they have walked into a two-hour mystery movie one hour after it started. All these cats! All those people! All those signs and ribbons on the cages! Whodunit? What *is* it they're doing? Why?

Having withstood the initial burst of sensory overload—"My *goodness*! I didn't know Persians' faces were so *flat*"—the first-time visitor begins to canvass the show hall, which may be anything from a musty armory to a high-dollar hotel or convention center. The most immediate attractions are the miles of aisles and cages filled with cats: cats with faces that come to a point, cats with faces that have no points; cats with folded ears, cats with curled ears; cats with bouffant hair, cats with shiny, slicked-down hair; cats with wavy hair, cats with no hair; massive cats, minuscule cats; solid-colored, bicolored, and tricolored cats; striped cats, spotted cats, mitted cats; and more than a few cats that look "just like Muffy at home."

The rows of cages are known as the benching area, the place where cats entered in the show are confined when they're not being judged. Visitors will be tempted to reach out and touch these exotic looking creatures. That's not a good idea. In their natural habitats cats are solitary creatures, and one of the best ways of challenging their immune systems is by bringing a large group of them together. An even better way is by bringing a large group of cats together and allowing persons to pet one cat and then to pet its neighbor down the aisle, thereby potentially spreading germs. Yet even though exhibitors don't want people touching the merchandise without permission, most exhibitors, especially if they've been winning that day, are happy to discuss their cat(s) with visitors and to tell them more—perhaps more than they ever wanted to know—about those cats when time permits.

If visitors are overcome with amazement at the mind boggling

The judging area. This judge is evaluating a beautifully groomed Persian.

It's one of life's infernal mysteries. Right up there with other cosmic questions such as why do we drive on parkways and park in driveways.

At any rate, in each ring—there can be as many as eight, even more—a judge stands behind a table, a row of 12 or so cages at his or her back. Spectators sitting in three or four rows of chairs watch the action. The judge takes each cat in turn from its cage, carries it to the judging table, examines it earnestly for a few moments, then returns it to the cage, usually hanging one or more ribbons on the cage afterward.

Thoroughly confused about how *this* works, visitors often wander off to browse the vendors who have come to the show like caravan merchants to display all manner of wares for cats and cat owners. At a show of any size or consequence these vendors proffer just about everything a cat owner could need, want, imagine, or buy on impulse— from $1.49 plastic litter scoops to $300 porcelain cat figurines. Some of the items we saw at a show recently included a wide variety of cat combs, brushes, shampoos and cleansers for a cat's face; vitamin supplements, rug cleaners, cat carriers, water dishes, feeding bowls and place mats, cat beds, myriad toys with and without catnip, leashes, coffee mugs, collector's plates, cat figurines, T-shirts, jewelry, key holders, greeting cards—the list is endless.

variety of cats on display at a show, they are awash with curiosity at the procedure in the judging rings. Those rings, which are actually rectangular in shape, are where the action is at a cat show—for exhibitors at least. Don't ask us why they're called rings.

At a cat show, you can indulge your urge to shop.

Such is a cat show. A ritual that is equal parts social gathering, art form, and shopping spree. We invite you, now, to have a look at a typical ring being judged at a typical cat show. We'll explain what the judge is looking for, what all those ribbons mean, and what the cheering is about.

A Ringside Seat

A cat show is actually a bunch of individual shows held separately but at the same time in several judging rings throughout the show hall. This is why a visitor to a cat show might hear someone say, "The show in Altoona next week is an eight-ring show." That means eight sets of awards will be offered, and eight cats—though not necessarily eight different ones—will be crowned best cat in show.

With few exceptions every cat in the hall is eligible to compete in every individual show or ring. Each show/ring is presided over by a different judge who presents awards independent of the decisions of other judges. Therefore, a cat chosen best in show by the judge in ring 1 may not receive the same award—or any award at all—from the judge in ring 2.

Each judge in every ring in the show hall evaluates cats according to a schedule, and the schedule is different from one judge to the next. The judge in ring 1 may begin with kittens, then go on to household pets, then proceed through the other competitive categories. The judge in ring 2 may begin with new breeds

and colors, then progress to altered cats, then kittens, and so forth.

Let's assume for purposes of demonstration that we are visiting a show licensed by the Cat Fanciers' Association (CFA), the world's largest pedigreed-cat registry. (One association licenses all the individual shows/rings that make up a cat show.) Let's further assume that we are watching a class of Persians being judged in championship competition. Championship competition is for pedigreed, unaltered, adult cats of either sex in the breeds recognized by CFA. An adult is a cat that is at least eight months old on the day of the show—or the opening day of the show if it's a two-day show. Two other types of competition exist at shows: nonchampion and alter (more on these later in this chapter).

A wide variety of toys and accessories can be purchased at cat shows. This shopper is testing the merchandise on her Abyssinian kitten before she buys.

Because there might be as many as 150 to 200 cats in the championship category, it would be difficult for a judge to evaluate one cat after another and then select the ten best cats in show—the selection of which is the final object of judging. Moreover, these top-ten places are not the only awards for which cats are competing. Cats also compete for winner's ribbons and/or points toward the various titles offered by cat associations. Therefore, cats are called to the ring by breeds. The ring clerks—the people sitting at either end of the judging table—are responsible for posting the cats' catalog numbers on top of the judging cages and for having the cats summoned to the ring in an orderly fashion via the public address system.

Just as a judge does not attempt to evaluate all championship cats en masse, neither are all members of a breed considered in that manner. Many breeds—the exceptions being those breeds that occur in only one color and those breeds that do not provide a lot of entries—are broken into divisions, which are groups of similar colors or patterns that occur within a breed. Those divisions can be further segregated into color classes. Judging begins at the color-class level within a breed and proceeds upward in a pyramid scheme.

Every cat in championship competition in CFA starts its show career in the open class, where it competes against other cats of the same breed, sex, and color for a first-place ribbon. (In the less-populous breeds, cats belonging to different color classes may compete against each other.) First-place ribbons are blue, second-place red, and third-place yellow.

A first-place blue award ribbon in the open class is accompanied by a red-white-and-blue winner's ribbon. Once a cat has collected six winner's ribbons, it becomes a champion. At its next show it is eligible to compete in the champion class against other champions for points toward the grand champion title.

After a judge has handled the open cats in a breed, division, or color grouping—and has awarded a winner's ribbon to the best male and the best female in that group—he judges the champions in that group. The judge then awards first-, second-, and third-place ribbons to the three best male and three best female champions. Next, the judge moves on to the grand champions and repeats that process.

When all the cats in a color group have been appraised, the judge awards the best of color class (black) and second best of color class (white) ribbons, which go to the cats in the group that meet the standard for their breed most closely.

After evaluating the white Persians, the judge proceeds to each of the other solid colors, awarding ribbons as before. (A judge may withhold a ribbon from any cat that does not possess sufficient merit or sufficient evidence of good health and/or grooming, but this does not happen frequently.) Then, having evaluated all the solid-colored Persians, which together constitute the solid-color Persian division, the judge reviews these cats and awards additional ribbons for best of division (brown), second best of division (orange), and best champion of division (purple). The best champion receives one point toward its grand championship title for each champion it defeated. Once a cat accumulates 200 points, it becomes a grand champion. (In the less-populous or single-color breeds that are not broken down into divisions, the judge awards best-of-breed, second-best-of-breed, and best-champion-of-breed ribbons.)

When all the solid-colored Persians have been assessed, the judge advances to the other divisions in the breed: tabby, particolor, and so on, until all Persians have been appraised. At that point another

The show ring. The judge brings each cat up to the judging area for evaluation. Behind, the cats wait in cages marked with each cat's number.

breed will be called to the ring. After a judge has examined all the cats in championship competition, it is time for finals: the curtain call wherein the judge presents the top ten cats in show. As a reverent hush envelops the crowd gathered about the ring, the judge introduces the cats in ascending order of merit until the best cat in show has been held aloft to the applause of the spectators. This is the moment every cat exhibitor lives for: a moment of exaltation and triumph that cat showing holds in common with all other competitive endeavors.

Kinds of Shows

Now that we've observed the underlying structure of a cat show, let's have a look at the different variations in which that structure can be found. The various individual shows/rings that make up a cat show can be divided into two types: allbreed and specialty.

Allbreed. Allbreed shows are exactly that—shows where cats of all breeds recognized by the association sanctioning the show are eligible to compete for awards.

Specialty. At specialty shows, entries are restricted to cats of similar coat length, breed, conformation, or color. For example, specialty shows are held for longhaired or shorthaired breeds only; for one specific breed, such as Siamese or Persian; and for breeds of similar type, such as all oriental breeds.

Competitive Categories

If you were constructing a cat show chart in your mind, the designations *allbreed* and *specialty*, which describe the kinds of shows offered,

The judge quickly but carefully evaluates each cat's merit according to the breed standard.

would constitute mutually exclusive, classifications: the vertical columns of the chart. In addition to those vertical columns, the kinds of shows can be divided horizontally into three competitive categories (or rows). These are championship, alter, and nonchampionship. The requirements for entering a cat or kitten in each of these competitive categories are subject to change. We have done our best to see that all the information presented in this book is correct at the time of printing. Nevertheless, we advise all novice exhibitors to obtain current show rules from any association in which they are interested in entering their cats (see Useful Addresses and Literature, page 125).

Championship competition. As we noted in the previous example, championship competition is for unaltered, pedigreed cats that are at least eight months old on the day of the show and are members of breeds accepted for championship competition in the association licensing the show.

Alter competition (called "premier" in CFA). Alter classes are for spayed or neutered adult cats that would, if they were whole (unaltered) cats, be eligible for championship competition. Many fanciers who do not breed cats (and some who do) show in the alter classes. Cats in alter classes are evaluated by the same breed standards that are used to appraise cats in championship classes.

Nonchampionship. This competitive category can be subdivided into five types: kitten, provisional (or new breed), household pet, any other variety, and miscellaneous.

Kitten competition is for pedigreed kittens between four months and one day less than eight months of age. The age of the kitten should be calculated for the day of the show, not the date on which you enter the kitten in the show. If your kitten is younger than eight months when you enter her in the show, but is older than eight months when the show is held, you will have to transfer her to the appropriate adult class the morning of the show.

Kittens are judged according to the same breed standards as adult cats are, but certain allowances can be made in judging kittens to compensate for changes that can be expected to occur when they reach adulthood. For example, a show-quality adult Burmese must be free of all distinct barring on the legs, but trace barring is permitted in kittens because these faint markings should fade with age. Of course, a kitten with fewer traces of bars should be preferred over a kitten with heavier barring, all other things being equal.

Although kittens compete for awards in their classes and for final awards in shows—and for national and regional awards as well—they cannot earn points toward any titles. Only adult cats competing in championship or alter classes can earn points toward titles.

Provisional (or new-breed) competition is for cats or kittens accepted for registration but not for championship competition. In some associations the classes in which these cats compete are called "provisional" classes. In other associations these classes are called "new breed and color" classes or simply "new breed." Before a new breed or a new color of an existing breed can be accepted for championship competition, it must be accepted for registration. The requirements for accepting a new breed or a new color within a recognized breed vary from association to association, and even when conditions are met, there's no guarantee the breed will be accepted.

When a "breed" is granted provisional or new breed and color status, members of that breed may compete for awards only in those new breed or provisional classes. They cannot compete in championship classes until the breed is accorded full championship status.

Any other variety (AOV) classes, offered in CCA, CFA, and CFF, are for any registered cat or kitten that would qualify for championship or alter competition but for the fact that it does not conform to its breed standard in some way, usually because of color, coat, or conformation. For example, a Manx whose tail is too long to qualify it for championship competition would be shown in this class rather than in the championship class. An AOV is eligible only for awards in the AOV class of its own breed. In CFA, for example, AOVs compete by gender for first-, second-, and third-best of color within the breed.

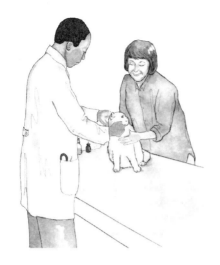

To enter a cat show, your cat should be in tip-top shape and needs up-to-date vaccinations. Schedule a visit with your veterinarian for a check up.

well enough to compete in the championship or alter classes successfully. In household pet (HHP) classes, which are offered in most but not all cat shows, cats are judged on their beauty, character, demeanor, and grooming rather than on a particular breed standard.

Cats must be at least four months old before they can be exhibited in the HHP kitten classes. Kittens do not have to be altered to be exhibited in these classes, but in every association an HHP must be altered in order to compete in adult classes, for which HHPs become eligible on the day they are eight months old.

Miscellaneous class, offered in CFA, is for breeds accepted for registration but not yet accepted for provisional breed competition. Entries in this class are examined by the judges but do not compete for awards. Miscellaneous classes are held to provide exposure for breeds whose proponents are hoping their cats will be granted provisional and championship status in the future. (CFA also has an exhibition-only designation for any cat or kitten that has been entered in the show but is not scheduled to be handled in any ring.)

Household pet classes are for mixed-breed cats or for purebred cats that don't meet their standards

A Cautionary Tale

Cats that compete in any kind of show—allbreed or specialty, championship or household pet—should be vaccinated, healthy, and free of fungus and parasites. In fact, any cats from houses or catteries where fungus or infectious illness has been present within three weeks of the show (four weeks in the American Association of Cat Enthusiasts) are ineligible for competition. Because the threat of contagion is very real at cat shows where so many cats are present, this is a wise precaution. Exhibitors don't want their cats picking up diseases along with their ribbons.

Chapter 2
A Brief History of the Cat Fancy

There are two means of refuge from the miseries of life: music and cats.
—Albert Schweitzer

Cat fancy is a term used to describe the group of people who breed or exhibit cats or both. *Confusing* is a word that can be used to describe the cat fancy. *Baffled* will do nicely to describe the would-be cat fancier. *Helpful* is what we hope this chapter will be.

Ten associations in North America register cats, train judges, sanction shows, and provide other services to cat fanciers. All ten associations have the same basic goals; nine of the ten contain the word *cat* in their names, and eight of those nine contain the word *association*. All are regularly referred to by their initials, which, because they contain only nine letters among them, look alike even though they have different meanings. Moreover, the rules, regulations, scoring procedures, and philosophies differ (sometimes greatly) from one association to the next. The novice exhibitor faced with choosing an association in which to register and to exhibit her cat, should know something about all these associations and about the history of the cat fancy.

Made in England

Although cats and humans had had a close relationship for thousands of years—some years, admittedly, were closer than others—no one thought to hold recurring contests to see whose cats were the cat's meow until the mid-1800s in

The first recorded cat show was held at the St. Giles Fair in England in 1598, the same year Shakespeare published Much Ado About Nothing.

A cat show in Britain. The cat fancy began in England and is immensely popular there today.

Britain. The earliest recorded cat show was held at the St. Giles Fair, Winchester, in 1598; but the first modern-day show was held in 1871 at the Crystal Palace in Sydenham, London. That show was the inspiration of Harrison Weir, a noted cat enthusiast whom many regard as the father of the cat fancy. Weir not only served on the panel of judges but also wrote the standards (then called "points of exhibition") by which the cats were evaluated. The Crystal Palace show featured Persians, Angoras, Russian Longhairs, British Shorthairs, and Siamese, among others. The Siamese were disparagingly described by a journalist of the day as "an unnatural, nightmare kind of cat." In all, roughly 160 cats were present at this groundbreaking affair, which was

such a success that exhibiting pedigreed cats suddenly became the rage du jour among the upper classes in the United Kingdom.

Weir helped to start the National Cat Club (NCC) in Britain in 1887, and was elected its first president. The NCC, whose motto was "Beauty Lives by Kindness," instituted the custom of recording the ancestors of cats in something called a stud book. This practice allowed exhibitors to verify that their cats were purebred and to govern, as much as these affairs lend themselves to governance, the physical appearance of future generations of cats.

The year after NCC had been established, The Cat Club (TCC), a rival organization, was founded. Because TCC maintained its own stud book and registry—and did not recognize registrations from NCC—cat fanciers were forced to show in one association only or to register their cats with both groups. Thus, from their very inception, cat associations lacked unity. Indeed, when additional cat clubs were started in England, most of them developed their own exclusive registration systems, too. This compounded the confusion because the various registration systems differed. Exhibitors who wanted to show their cats in more than one association had a lot of paperwork to keep track of and a lot of rules and regulations to learn—just as they do in the United States today. Finally, in 1910, the representatives of NCC met with the officers of the other clubs and developed the Governing Council of the Cat Fancy (GCCF), which keeps one central breed registry, licenses and regulates cat shows, looks after the welfare of cats, ensures that cat fancy rules are not broken, and eliminates the need for multiple registrations.

Cat Fancy Fever in the United States

American cat lovers, emulating their British counterparts, soon caught the cat fancy fever. By the 1870s cat shows were held in New England, where Maine Coon Cats were the featured and numerically superior contestants. Owners of Maine Coons kept pedigree records long before cat registries were

At British cat shows, the judge, accompanied by a steward, visits each cat's cage. No cage decorations are allowed for this reason, and the owners' names may not be placed on the cages so as not to sway the judges' opinions.

formed in this country around the turn of the century. In fact, a black-and-white Maine Coon named Captain Jenks of the Horse Marines was mentioned in popular literature as early as 1861.

An Englishman named James Hyde organized the first official cat show in the United States, held in May 1895 in New York's Madison Square Garden. A Maine Coon was best cat at that show, but the increasing popularity and importation of Persians and Siamese sent the Maine Coon into an exile from which it would not return for more than three quarters of a century.

The Madison Square Garden show is a convenient marker for the beginning of the developing cat fancy in America. When that fancy was born, no cat registries existed in this country, and stud books were kept for a time by a branch of the government.

Entries dropped from 176 at the first Madison Square Garden show to 130 the following year. Nevertheless, at the close of the 1896 show a group of cat fanciers created the American Cat Club, the first registry in the United States. The club was formed to verify pedigrees, maintain a stud book, sponsor shows, and promote the welfare of cats.

The American Cat Club was disbanded a year after it had been formed, and for several years there were no shows at Madison Square Garden. Meanwhile, cat fanciers in Chicago organized two clubs in 1899. The first was the Chicago Cat Club, which was followed and eventually overshadowed by the Beresford Club.

At British shows, the steward removes the cat from each cage and places it on a movable trolley so the judge can more easily evaluate each cat.

The Beresford Club, with a national membership of 170, began sponsoring shows in 1900, and in that year published the first stud book and register in the United States. The club's objectives were protecting the humane society and caring for all homeless or distressed cats, issues in which more of today's cat clubs should be involved. (Many cat clubs today are at odds with humane societies over differences of opinion regarding cat overpopulation and animal control ordinances.)

Though the Beresford Club continued to put on shows, it eventually ceased to function as a registering body. That task was taken over by the American Cat Association (ACA), generally referred to as the oldest cat registry in the United States. ACA, founded in 1899, was incorporated on May 11, 1904. Its first president, Mrs. Clinton Locke, had been importing and breeding cats since the late 1870s. She was the first woman in the United States to operate a cattery (an area, usually in the breeder's home, where cats are housed and bred).

Throughout this century a number of cat associations have been formed, most often because of differences of opinion between two factions of an existing group over how that association should be run. In 1906 a dissident faction of ACA members left that organization to form the Cat Fanciers' Association (CFA). In early 1919 when CFA refused to honor championship claims from certain exhibitors who were charged with violating show rules, the Silver Society, a CFA club, resigned. The Atlantic Cat Club, which had formerly resigned from ACA, now resigned from CFA and joined ranks with members of the Silver Society to organize the United Cat Fanciers Association, whose name was changed to the Cat Fanciers' Federation a few months later.

The Depression and the Second World War didn't leave much room for cat fancy maneuvering. By 1954, however, the National Cat Fanciers' Association had been formed, and the following year a group of CFA members who were not satisfied with the association's republican form of government left to start the American Cat Fanciers Association (ACFA). Twenty-four years later ACFA would give birth by fission to The International Cat Association (TICA).

The Cat Fancy Today

Because of the number of cat registries that exist today, the situation facing the novice fancier is more complicated than it was when the cat fancy began. At the time of this writing (spring 1998), there were ten cat registries in North America:

American Association of Cat Enthusiasts (AACE)
American Cat Association (ACA)
American Cat Fanciers Association (ACFA)
Canadian Cat Association (CCA)
Cat Fanciers' Association (CFA)
Cat Fanciers' Federation (CFF)
National Cat Fanciers' Association (NCFA)
The International Cat Association (TICA)
Traditional Cat Association (TCA)
United Feline Organization (UFO)

Clubs affiliated with these groups, after obtaining a show license from the parent organization, hold shows conducted in accordance with the rules of that association. Despite the differences between the associations, all share the same stated goals—the promotion and welfare of all cats and the improvement and preservation of recognized cat breeds. They keep stud books and records, maintain breed standards, register pedigreed cats, sanction shows, grant titles, keep track of points earned by cats at shows, provide information for breeders and training for clerks and judges, produce lectures and publications for their members, and educate cat owners.

Record keeping is one of the most important functions of the various associations. The purpose of registering purebred cats is to give breeders a continuing history of their breeds and to ensure that pedigrees are as accurate as possible and, hence, breeds are as purebred as it is possible to keep them.

The American Cat Association, as we have seen, is the oldest existing

registry. Today it is no longer a national association in scope, but holds most of its shows in Southern California. Cat fanciers wishing to join the association may do so directly or through one of its member clubs.

The Cat Fanciers' Association, formed in 1906 and incorporated in 1919, has grown into the largest cat registering body in the world. It includes more than 650 member clubs that produced 429 shows in the 1996-1997 show season. CFA also works closely with the Federation Internationale Feline, an international organization that oversees European and Australian cat associations. CFA does not offer individual memberships. Fanciers wishing to join CFA can join one of its member clubs, each of which sends an elected delegate to vote on rule changes and other matters at the association's annual meeting each year.

The Cat Fanciers' Federation (CFF), formed in 1919, currently has about 90 affiliated clubs. Most of those clubs are located in the Northeast, and, therefore, most CFF shows are held in that area. In the past cat fanciers joined CFF-affiliated clubs rather than the association itself, but recently the association instituted a policy by which individuals can become members of CFF.

The American Cat Fanciers Association (ACFA) was formed in 1955 in the Dallas-Fort Worth area. Its main office is now in Point Lookout, Missouri. The association's originators wanted to establish a democratic form of management in which members must approve changes in show or registration rules. Therefore, ACFA offers direct memberships in the association. ACFA was the first cat registry to provide classes in which altered cats could compete and the first to require judges to pass written exams before becoming licensed.

The Canadian Cat Association, formed in 1961, is the only Canadian registry. Its affiliated clubs hold shows across Canada, and it maintains a stud book for its members. The association, which people can join directly or through its member clubs, holds most of its shows in Ontario and Quebec.

The International Cat Association (TICA), the second-largest cat association in North America, originated in 1979. Located in Harlingen, Texas, it has additional charters in Argentina, Brazil, Canada, France, Japan, the Philippines, Singapore, and Switzerland. TICA is known as a genetic registry because it registers cats according to their genetic makeup rather than their appearance. In other words, if a Himalayan cat has Persian in its background, its registration number reveals the Persian ancestry. (However, cats competing in TICA shows are grouped according to physical appearance.) TICA also adopted a policy by which the judges' books at shows contain no information about cats' titles; this rule is designed to eliminate bias toward cats that have accumulated titles in previous shows. TICA is governed by a democratic arrangement in which every member is eligible to vote directly on show rules and other procedural matters.

The National Cat Fanciers' Association (NCFA), originally started in 1954, was registered as a nonprofit corporation in 1961. Because of its founder's illness in 1981, NCFA didn't renew its nonprofit status, and in 1990 the corporation was dissolved. It was reformed in 1991 and is continuing its objectives of furthering the enhancement of the natural beauty of the purebred cat while retaining the cat's lovable personality. Its emphasis is on being a family-oriented association, and it encourages young people to participate in showing cats by holding shows at 4-H meetings and fairs. Its main office is in Brant, Michigan. NCFA is the only association that has fun show classes: These are classes in which purebred cats compete for prizes awarded to best coat (long and short), most aloof, most lovable, classiest cat, most feminine, most masculine, most comical, and most talented. There is also a costume class for purebreds. Household pets, for their part, can compete in fun classes that determine the most unusual cat, fattest cat, most playful cat, best lap cat, cat with the biggest paws, and so on. Anyone registering a cat with NCFA automatically becomes a member of the association.

The Traditional Cat Association (TCA) was founded in 1987. It strives to preserve, protect, perpetuate, and promote traditional cats—those cats whose body styles and conformation types have given way to different, usually more extreme, forms in some of the other associations. It recognizes the following breeds: Traditional Siamese (also called Old Style or Applehead Siamese), Classic Siamese, Traditional Balinese, Classic Balinese, Authentic Bengal, Colorpoint Shorthair, Traditional Burmese, Classic Burmese, Original Himalayan and Traditional Persian (also called the Doll-Face), Nebelung, the North American Tiffany, and household pets. The association keeps a stud book of both purebred and household pets. TCA sponsors shows and offers people the option of joining the association directly or one of its member clubs.

The American Association of Cat Enthusiasts (AACE) was formed in 1993. Its goal is to make sure the exhibitors get a fair appraisal of their cats while having fun in the process, something that members claim was missing in some of the other associations. (Other associations, of course, might have a different opinion on those matters.) AACE membership can be obtained by joining the association directly or through joining one of its member clubs.

The United Feline Organization (UFO), located in Olympia, Washington, was the newest cat registering association at the time of this writing. Its goal is to "go where no cat organization has gone before." It is dedicated to creating an association that, by a system of checks and balances, will prevent the kind of strife that members have found objectionable in other associations. UFO offers individual and club memberships. Individual members vote for candidates running for office and on proposed bylaws to the group's constitution. Clubs vote on show rules.

Chapter 3
Choosing a Breed

The great thing about cats is their endless variety. One can pick a cat to fit almost any kind of decor, color scheme, income, personality, mood. But under the fur, whatever color it may be, there still lies, essentially unchanged, one of the world's free souls.

—Eric Gurney

Which breed is right for you? Well, that depends on a number of factors. If exhibiting your cat is an important goal, you need to consider carefully before selecting a breed. The following chapter will give you basic information on many of the breeds accepted by today's cat associations, but ultimately your personal tastes must be considered when selecting a breed. Don't choose a breed you don't find attractive, just because you think it will do well in the shows. Choose a breed that appeals to your tastes and lifestyle first—then judge its potential in the show ring. Because cats are aesthetically appealing, some people may think of them as furry works of art; but cats are living, sentient beings, not couch ornaments or—worse—cage potatoes. They must

be respected as living beings if your experience with them is to be a positive one. After all, after the show is over you'll be going home together, and you want that time to be precious, too.

Therefore, it's important to learn all you can about a breed before agreeing to buy. Make sure you know all about the breed's conformation, traits, and temperament. The best way to become acquainted with the purebreds available to today's fancier is to go to cat shows and talk to breeders and exhibitors. Ask how well their cats perform in the ring and whether they enjoy showing this particular breed. Ask about the breed's pros and cons. You'll learn a lot from their comments.

Long Hair or Short?

Cats are generally divided into two groups on the basis of coat length—longhair and shorthair; but virtually all cats, except some Rex breeds and the Sphynx, have three kinds of hairs: guard, awn, and down. The guard hairs, which are the least numerous of the three, are long

Considerable differences exist in the texture, length, and density of cats' coats. For example, the Persian's coat has been refined so that the down hairs are almost as long as the guard hairs, giving the coat a particularly soft, silky texture. A Persian's fur can be as much as eight inches long, and a show Persian requires daily grooming to keep that fur looking its best. Persians need frequent grooming when not being shown, too. Other longhaired breeds, such as the Angora and Balinese, have silky coats lacking for the most part the easily matted downy undercoat; therefore, they require less grooming.

When you are showing cats, grooming is a given no matter what breed you buy, but shorthaired cats generally require less grooming than longhaired breeds. If your free time is limited and you cannot give a longhaired cat the grooming attention it needs, select a shorthaired breed, one that possesses traits similar to those of the longhaired breed you like. The Exotic Shorthair, for example, has a body style and personality similar to the Persian's, but the Exotic has a short coat that's easier to keep groomed.

and stiff. They constitute the top layer of the cat's coat. Guard hairs help to keep a cat dry and to protect the softer underlying hairs. The down and awn hairs are called the secondary hairs or the undercoat. They are more plentiful than the protective guard hairs. The awn hairs, which make up the middle layer of a cat's coat, are thin and usually have stiff pointed ends. The baby-fine down hairs, the layer of the coat closest to the skin, are soft and wavy. The down hairs are the most numerous hairs in a cat's coat. They also are the hairs that mat the easiest.

The thickness and length of a cat's coat change from season to season, typically reaching the heaviest texture and longest length in the winter. In the fall, the summer coat is shed and the awn and down hairs become more abundant in order to provide warmth and insulation in preparation for winter. In the spring, the thicker undercoat is shed to prepare for the warm season.

Conformation

Conformation, also called *type*, refers to the physical appearance of a cat. The appropriate type for each breed is specified in the breed standards of the various cat associations. Standards define the ideal characteristics for each breed: body, color, pattern, eye color, shape, and set, ear size, shape, and set, and so on. Most breeds can be classified as cobby, foreign, or moderate. The cobby body design is short and compact, deep chested, and broad across the shoulders and rump. The head is large and round, the muzzle short, and the tail is usually shorter and thicker than in other breeds. Persians, Exotics, and Himalayans are cobby breeds.

The foreign body type is slim and svelte with long, tapering lines. The head is narrow and pointy and usually wedge shaped. Siamese, Balinese, and Oriental cats are foreign in type.

The third body type, moderate, lies somewhere between cobby and foreign. The American Curl and Havana Brown are examples of moderate conformation.

The body type that suits you best depends entirely on your sense of aesthetics. Some people love the heavy, rounded body of the Persian. Others prefer the lithe, elegant lines of the Siamese. The best way to get a good feel for the breeds available is to take in a few cat shows. Wander among the cages and see which breeds appeal to you.

Abyssinians are the second most popular shorthaired breed. They are affectionate, beautiful, and lovable—and active. Before choosing this breed, be sure you have the time to devote to their special needs.

Temperament Considerations

A cat's packaging is not the only consideration. You must also consider contents: a breed's activity level and temperament. An active breed such as the Abyssinian, Cornish Rex, or Bengal may annoy you if you aren't fascinated by its constant explorations and requests for attention. Conversely, a docile breed such as the Persian or Himalayan may bore you if you like a frisky, energetic companion.

A breed's vocal tendencies are another important consideration. Some breeds will drive you crazy if you crave peace and quiet. People who believe cats should be seen but not heard should avoid the Siamese and all breeds that have Siamese in their backgrounds. These cats tend to enjoy a good conversation with their human companions—or with themselves.

Some breeds—including the Bombay, Burmese, Siamese and its

Some breeds require more attention than others and will miss you when you're away from home. Be sure you have the time to devote to your cat.

related breeds—need more attention than others, and this, too, is an important consideration. The need for attention is not a negative trait, but if you travel a lot or work long hours, it's best to choose a less dependent breed, one that won't miss you so dramatically when you go away. Of course, providing a feline companion for your cat can help in that regard.

Breed Profiles

The following breed profiles will give you a brief description of the personality, history, and conformation of each breed accepted for championship competition by at least one cat association in North America at the time of this writing (spring 1998). The list does not include descriptions of experimental or provisional breeds not yet accepted for championship classes in any association.

Abyssinian. The Abyssinian is an energetic, lively breed, known for its playful antics. Vocally it is quiet. A shorthaired, colorful, regal cat, the Abyssinian resembles cats worshiped in the temples and palaces of the ancient Egyptians some 4,000 years ago. It is slim, lithe, and graceful with strikingly large ears and large, expressive, almond-shaped eyes. The Aby's distinctive ticked coat has alternating bands of colors on each hair shaft. Ruddy, red (sometimes called sorrel), blue, and fawn are the most frequently seen Abyssinian colors, but some registries also accept silver Abys and their associated color variations. Although generally healthy, the Abyssinian is susceptible to gingivitis and to higher than usual incidents of amyloidosis, a fatal renal disease. The Abyssinian is accepted in all associations.

American Curl. Curls are gentle and devoted to their human companions, but have a playful side as well. The Curl's unique ears curl back on its head, giving the cat a whimsical appearance.

The first American Curl, Shulamith, was a stray who appeared on the doorstep of a Southern California couple in 1981. Although Shulamith was a longhair, shorthair genes were soon added to the bloodline, establishing both hair lengths early in the breed's development. The unusual ear arrangement is governed by a dominant gene (if a kitten inherits one gene for regular ears and the other for curled ears, its ears will be curled). The curl-ear gene does not appear to be associated with any harmful defects. Curls are slender, well-balanced, and moderately muscled cats with a moderate body style. The Curl is accepted in every color and pattern, including the Siamese pattern. This breed has championship status in all associations.

American Shorthair. An easygoing breed, the American Shorthair is perfect for those who seek a feline companion that doesn't need constant attention. Moderately active, the American Shorthair enjoys playing and generally doesn't like to be held and cuddled. The breed arose largely from the domestic cat population, with a midcentury assist from some clandestine Persian breedings. It is a powerful, solidly built, muscular cat with well-developed shoulders, chest, and hindquarters. American Shorthairs come in an abundance of colors, the most popular being the silver tabby, which accounts for more than one third of the total breed population. The American Shorthair, generally a hardy, healthy breed, is accepted for championship competition by all associations.

American Wirehair. Because this rare breed is still developing, its personality may vary from one cattery to the next. In general, however, the American Wirehair is a sweet, loving, gregarious cat with an outgoing temperament and a love of play.

The first American Wirehair kitten appeared in 1966 in a litter of normal-coated barn cats in Verona, New

York. A breeder named Joan O'Shea acquired that kitten. She crossed it with domestic shorthairs and eventually developed the Wirehair into a recognized breed. The Wirehair's distinctive look comes from a coat mutation governed by a dominant gene that creates a short, wiry coat. Each individual hair is hooked, crimped, or bent, including the whiskers and the hair in the ears. The breed comes in all colors except chocolate and lavender and in all patterns except Siamese. It has championship status in ACA, ACFA, CCA, CFA, TICA, and UFO.

Balinese. Balinese are active, talkative extroverts. Like the Siamese, they are never at a loss for words and are highly social and dependent upon their human companions. Named after the graceful dancers from the Isle of Bali, this cat is essentially a longhaired Siamese.

The Birman— sacred cat of Burma.

Cornish Rex cats.

Longhaired kittens began appearing in Siamese litters in the early 1900s. Some breeders theorize that the longhair gene was introduced into Siamese bloodlines in Europe after World War I. As early as the 1950s breeders began working to get the Balinese recognized as a distinct breed. The Balinese body style is identical to that of the Siamese, but the coat is semilong and easy to care for because it lacks the easily matted downy undercoat that plagues some longhaired breeds and their owners. In CFA the breed is recognized in seal, blue, chocolate, and lilac; but in AACE, ACA, ACFA, CCA, CFF, TICA, and UFO the Balinese is also accepted in red, cream, torte, and lynx points. In CFA, cats with these colors are called Javanese. The breed, by whatever name, has championship status in all associations.

Bengal. Bengals are lively, active cats with a healthy dose of curiosity, strong hunting instincts, and high intelligence. One of four spotted breeds currently seen at cat shows, the Bengal was conceived in this country in 1963 from a cross between a female Asian leopard cat (*Felis bengalensis*) and a male domestic shorthair. Some cat fanciers are concerned that the "wild" blood may cause temperament problems in the Bengal. Therefore, in the interest of ensuring a milder, more docile temperament, associations may require Bengal-to-Bengal breedings for at least four generations before cats can be shown. The Bengal is a large, sleek, shorthaired, beautifully spotted cat with a feral, exotic look. The spots, which contrast with the background color, can be black, brown, tan, chocolate, or cinnamon. (Bengals are also accepted in a marble pattern in a few associations.) The breed has championship status in TICA, CCA, UFO, and TCA. At the time of this writing it had provisional status in CFF and registration status in ACFA, but it could not be shown in the latter association.

Birman. Birmans are affectionate, gentle, sweet-tempered, faithful companions that have an air of quiet dignity about them. According to breed legend, the Birman, also called the Sacred Cat of Burma, is descended from cats revered in the Buddhist temples of Burma. These cats were thought to carry the souls of priests who had died into the next world.

The Birman is a pointed-pattern cat with long, silky hair and a strongly built, stocky, elongated body. Its eyes are a brilliant blue and its feet are white. CFA recognizes the breed in seal, blue, chocolate, and lilac, but other associations accept a more adventuresome range of colors. Birmans have championship status in all associations.

Bombay. The Bombay, which is similar in personality and conformation to the Burmese (see below), is active, playful, talkative, and affectionate. Bombays crave constant attention and tend to follow your every move. According to official accounts, the Bombay was developed from deliberate crosses between sable Burmese and black American Shorthairs in an attempt to create a "mini black panther."

Bombays have large, rounded expressive eyes, a pleasingly rounded head with a sweet facial expression, a compact, muscular body, a short, sleek, gleaming black coat, and glowing copper eyes. They enjoy championship status in all associations.

British Shorthair. British Shorthairs are quiet, undemanding companions. They were developed from street cats once called European Shorthairs that were brought to Great Britain by the Romans some 2,000 years ago. The breed is a large, powerful teddy bear of a cat with a round face and large, round eyes. Full cheeks give the British a perpetual smile. Its short coat is dense and firm to the touch. While blue is the most common color, the breed comes in a profusion of other colors and patterns including tabby, smoke, tortoiseshell, calico, and bicolor. The British Shorthair has championship status in all associations.

Burmese. Burmese are curious, active, and emotionally attached to their owners. They have a unique, raspy voice and can be talkative when they have something to say. The American Burmese is descended from a brown female cat named Wong Mau brought to the United States from Yangon, Myanmar, in 1930. Shorthaired, brown cats of her type have abounded in Southeast Asia for centuries. Today's Burmese is a shorthaired, medium-sized, muscular cat that is surprisingly heavy for its size.

Three conformation types exist—the European Burmese, which has a longer, narrower muzzle with a less pronounced nose break and a slightly narrower head, the contemporary Burmese, which has a shorter, broader muzzle, pronounced nose break, and broader, rounder head, and the Traditional Burmese, which looks more like the breed did when it was first developed—less cobby and with a longer muzzle. In CFA the European Burmese has just been accepted as a breed in its own right in the miscellaneous class. This class does not enjoy championship in the United States, though it does in CFA's international-division shows. In CFF, CCA, and UFO the breed is recognized under the name Foreign

The Exotic Shorthair, called the Exotic by some associations, is basically a shorthaired Persian.

Burmese. TCA recognizes the Traditional Burmese and the Classic Burmese. In most associations the Burmese, which enjoys championship status throughout the fancy, comes in four colors: sable, champagne, blue, and platinum, but the European Burmese comes in additional colors. Although the Burmese is generally healthy, the extreme shortening of the nose in some contemporary bloodlines is believed to be associated with cranial birth defects.

Chartreux. These cats are amiable, loyal, and quiet. The Chartreux is often described as one of the "oldest new breeds." Allegedly, the Chartreux developed at the Le Grand Chartreux monastery in the French Alps outside Paris. As the story goes, the Carthusian order of

monks at the monastery selectively bred the Chartreux to have quiet voices, so the cats would not disturb their meditations. Appealing as this sounds, we are obliged to point out that Carthusian archives do not mention blue cats or cats of any other color.

The breed as we know it today was rediscovered on the small Brittany island of Belle-lle-sur-Mere off the northwest coast of France. Cat show records reveal that a Mlle. Leger was the first person to exhibit Chartreux in France, at a show in Paris in 1931. Mlle. Leger and her sister also bred Persians and Siamese in their de Guerveur Cattery. They moved from the mainland to Belle-lle-sur-Mere in the late 1920s, and shortly after they had arrived on the island, they discovered a bountiful population of blue-gray cats in Le Palais, the island's principal city. Since many of these roaming cats hung around the hospital in Le Palais, they were known in that vicinity as hospital cats.

The Chartreux is sometimes unflatteringly called a "potato on toothpicks" because of its stocky body and slender legs, but it is nevertheless extremely agile and graceful. The head is round and broad, and the breed is known for the way it seems to smile. The coat is medium-short and slightly wooly. The breed comes in only one color—blue—but the shade can range from ash to slate. Generally the Chartreux is a healthy and hardy breed, but some lines possess the recessive gene for medial patellar luxation. It has championship status in all associations.

Cornish Rex. Cornish Rexes are active, spirited, agile, and affectionate. They can be hard to ignore when they're in a sociable mood—which is most of the time.

The first known Cornish Rex was discovered in an otherwise normal litter of kittens in 1950 on a farm in Bodmin Moor, Cornwall, England. Because of the influence of a recessive mutation, the Cornish coat lacks guard hairs; and the down and awn hairs are soft, wavy, and curly. The coat feels like warm suede to the touch. Contrary to rumor, this breed is not hypoallergenic (nor is any other breed). The Cornish Rex has been compared to the Whippet because of its lean, racy build. The back is naturally arched, and the cat stands high on its legs. The ears and eyes are large. The Cornish Rex is available in virtually every color and pattern, including the pointed pattern called the "Si-Rex." It has championship status in all associations.

Devon Rex. Devon Rexes are animated, affectionate, and intelligent. They tend to be vocally quiet, but they take an active interest in their surroundings and their favorite humans.

The origin of the Devon Rex breed can be traced to 1960 to a feral, curly-coated tom that lived around an abandoned tin mine near Devon, England. This breed's recessive coat mutation is similar to the Cornish Rex's, but the coats are not identical. Because of the influence of the Devon gene, all three hair types are very short with tight, curly waves. For this reason the Devon is sometimes called "the poodle cat." Devons have jumbo-sized, satellite dish ears and large eyes, creating a characteristic elfin look. Devon Rexes are available in virtually any color or pattern. They have championship status in all associations.

Egyptian Mau. Egyptian Maus are active, athletic cats that are fiercely loyal to their human companions but wary of strangers. The breed originated in Egypt, where spotted cats matching the Mau's description can be found in Egyptian paintings and sculptures dating to 2000 B.C. The only natural breed of spotted domestic cat, the Mau is a long, graceful, muscular cat with a stride like a cheetah. A loose flap of skin extends from the flank to the back knee, which allows for greater length of stride and agility. The coat is medium long with a lustrous sheen. Three colors are universally accepted—silver, bronze, and black smoke. The eyes are gooseberry green. The Mau has championship status in all associations.

Exotic Shorthair. Like the Persian, the Exotic Shorthair is docile, sweet, affectionate, and agreeable. Because of the American Shorthair influence, Exotics are somewhat more active than Persians.

Known simply as the Exotic in CCA and CFA, this breed was developed in the United States in the 1960s when breeders crossed American Shorthairs with Persians in order to improve type in American Shorthairs. The Exotic's body and head type are identical to the Persian's, but the Exotic possesses a short, plush coat that makes grooming much easier. The breed comes in all of the Persian colors and patterns, including the pointed pattern. It has championship status in all associations.

Because Persians are an allowable outcross for Exotic Shorthairs, not all Exotics have short hair. In some associations Longhaired Exotics cannot be shown, in others they are either shown as Persians or as a separate breed.

Havana Brown. Havana Browns are affectionate, adaptable, gentle, highly intelligent, and quiet. They are remarkably agreeable cats and adjust to any situation with poise and confidence. Havanas must have lots of human interaction if they are to live happy lives.

A solid brown cat the color of rich chocolate, the Havana Brown was transported to England from Thailand (then Siam) around the same time as the Siamese in the latter part of the 19th century. The Havana has a body that falls midway between the cobby and the svelte breeds. Its distinctive corncob muzzle, brilliant, expressive oval eyes, and large, wide-set ears give the cat a unique appearance. Its coat is short, smooth, and lustrous, and is an even shade of brown throughout. Havana Browns enjoy championship status in all associations, some of which also accept Havanas in lavender as well as brown.

Himalayan. Like Persians, Himalayans are docile, calm, and sweet-tempered, but they possess a playful side as well. Although they have Siamese in their backgrounds, they are generally not vocal.

The Himalayan was created in the 1950s by a trio of breeders— one British, one American, and one Canadian—who wanted to create a cat with the Persian body style and the Siamese color pattern. The Himalayan's body, coat length, and head type are identical to the Persian's, but Himmys possess the pointed pattern (i.e., the mask, ears, legs, feet, and tail are darker than the rest of the body). The coat can be as much as eight inches long. Himalayan colors include seal, chocolate, blue, lilac, flame (red), cream, blue-cream, lilac-cream, tortoiseshell, lynx, and torte-lynx varieties. In some associations the Himalayan is considered a division of the Persian rather than a separate breed, but Himalayans by whatever designation are accepted in all associations.

Japanese Bobtail. Japanese Bobtails are curious, active, intelligent, and alert. They usually adapt well to new people and to new environments. Bobtails are fairly vocal and have chirping voices that produce a wide range of tones. Some breeders describe this as "singing."

The Japanese Bobtail has been held in high esteem for centuries in its native land. The first documented Japanese Bobtails were imported into the United States from Japan in 1908, but it wasn't until 1968 that a formal breeding program began in this country. The Japanese Bobtail is a lean, elegant cat with large ears and eyes and a distinctively short pompom tail. The recessive Bobtail gene doesn't appear to be associated with any genetic defects and is not related to the Manx gene. Bobtails are recognized in both long and shorthaired varieties and in many colors and patterns, but the most common is the tricolor or "mi-ke" pattern, in which the cat is mostly white with patches of red, cream, and black. Japanese Bobtails, the shorthaired variety at least, have championship status in all associations. Longhaired Bobtails are not yet universally accepted.

Korat. Korats are not as vocal as some breeds, but they will speak their minds if something is amiss. They are energetic, intelligent, social, and affectionate, and particularly enjoy games in which you take an active part.

Korats are native to Siam (now Thailand), where they are considered symbols of good luck. The breed first arrived in the United States in 1959. The Korat is a shorthaired, moderate breed, neither compact nor svelte. Its large ears, which sit high on its head, give the Korat an alert expression, which is complemented by large eyes of brilliant, luminous green. Korats come in one color only—solid silver blue. Each hair is tipped with silver, which produces a shimmering halo effect. Korats have championship status in all associations.

Maine Coon Cat. Maine Coon cats are adaptable, good-tempered, and gentle, and get along well with people and animals. They tend to form a close bond with one member of the household and become completely devoted to that person.

The ancestors of the Maine Coon arrived in America with the European colonists sometime in the 1600s or 1700s. Through natural selection the Maine Coon developed into a large, hardy cat with a long, dense, water-resistant coat and a healthy constitution. One of the largest breeds of domestic cat, the Maine Coon is muscular and broad-chested with brawny legs and large, well-tufted paws. The brown tabby is the most common color and pattern, but any color or pattern is acceptable, save those that indicate hybridization (e.g., pointed patterns or colors). Maine Coons have championship status in all associations.

Manx. Manx cats are intelligent, moderately active, and love to play. Their powerful hind legs make them exceptional jumpers. The Manx's defining trait is its lack of a tail, the result of a natural dominant mutation thought to have developed on the Isle of Man. In reality, the Manx gene does not always produce tailless cats; and Manx can have tails of various lengths that are usually classified as one of four types: rumpy, rumpy-riser, stumpy, and longy. The rumpy, which is entirely tailless, is the Manx seen in the show ring. Compact, muscular, and round, Manx occur in long and shorthaired varieties. The Longhaired Manx is called the Cymric in some associations. All colors and patterns are acceptable, save those that suggest hybridization, such as the Siamese pointed pattern. The Manx gene is known to cause deformities such as Spina bifida, fusions of the spine, and defects of the colon. Moreover, kittens that inherit two Manx genes fail to develop in the womb. The breed, nevertheless, has championship status in all associations.

Nebelung. The Nebelung is a shy but affectionate breed. Sweet and loving, Nebelungs form close bonds with their human companions and stay devoted and loyal their entire lives. The breed's name (pronounced NAY-bel-ung), is a German word that translates to "creature of the mist," an appropriate name for a feline that vanishes into thin air when strangers come to visit.

The Nebelung was developed in the 1980s from a chance mating between a shorthaired black domestic named Elsa and a shorthaired Russian Blue-type tomcat. Owned by cat lover Cora Cobb, Elsa produced a litter that included one longhaired blue male kitten. This kitten, which Cobb named Siegfried after the hero in her favorite Wagner opera cycle "The Ring of the Nibelung," was destined to become the father of the Nebelung breed.

Elsa's next litter included a longhaired, blue female kitten that looked like Siegfried, which Cobb named Brunhilde. By breeding Siegfried to Brunhilde, Cobb began the Nebelung breed. To increase the gene pool and improve the body type so the Nebelung could more closely resemble the standard suggested by TICA's geneticist (who Cobb asked for advice), Cobb outcrossed the kittens to purebred Russian Blues. Russian Blues played an important role in the development of this breed, and today the Nebelung and Russian Blue breeds share a common conformation—the difference is the coat length. The Nebelung is a beautiful breed, with a semilong, luminous blue coat tipped with silver, snapping green eyes, and a long, elegant "foreign" body. Even though the Nebelung is essentially a longhaired Russian Blue, TICA recognizes it as a breed in its own right and accepts it for championship status.

Norwegian Forest Cat. Wegies, as they are often called, are family oriented, active, and playful, and retain their affectionate, fun-loving spirit into adulthood. Natural athletes, Norwegian Forest Cats love to investigate the tops of bookcases and refrigerators.

A large, hardy, natural breed that has existed in Norway for hundreds of years, the Wegie didn't arrive in the United States until 1980. This powerful, solidly muscled cat with substantial bone structure has a long, heavy coat, a lush mane, and a majestic appearance. Brown tabbies, silver tabbies, and tabbies with white patches are the most common colors and pattern combinations, but all colors and patterns are acceptable as long as they do not indicate hybridization (e.g., Siamese colors or patterns). Forest cats have championship status in all associations.

Ocicat. Ocicats are active, affectionate, and people oriented. They are inclined to bond with just one person and to prefer that person's company to all others. Possessing a keen intelligence, Ocicats quickly learn to respond to their names, and can be taught a variety of tricks. Like the Siamese, who is one of their ancestors, they can be quite vocal.

The Ocicat is a spotted domestic breed that looks like a wild cat. It was first developed in the United States in 1964 from crosses between ruddy Abyssinians and Sealpoint and chocolate point Siamese. Later, American Shorthairs were added to the mix. The breed is large, athletic,

graceful, lithe, and long-bodied with substantial bone and muscle development. The coat is short, bears Abyssinian-style ticking, and possesses round or thumbprint-shaped spots. The forehead bears the classic tabby "M." The Ocicat comes in a variety of colors including tawny, chocolate, cinnamon, blue, lavender, fawn, and silver. It has championship status in all associations.

(above) Norwegian Forest Cat.

(below) Ocicat. This breed was created by crossing Abyssinians, Siamese, and American Shorthairs.

White Oriental Shorthairs. These cats have the same body type as the Siamese.

KITTENS FOR SALE

Oriental. Orientals (known in some associations as Oriental Shorthairs) are active, loving, and intelligent. Extremely people oriented and trusting, they crave human attention and show an almost doglike dependence on their owners. They can also be quite vocal.

A close relative of the Siamese, the Oriental was developed in the 1950s and 1960s when breeders in Britain and America crossed Siamese cats with domestic shorthairs, Russian Blues, and Abyssinians. This breed has the same type as the Siamese—svelte with long, tapering lines, strikingly large, pointed ears and almond-shaped slanting eyes—but comes in more

than 300 color and pattern combinations. Orientals are available in both long and shorthaired varieties; the Oriental Longhair is not accepted in all associations. In CFA, both varieties are recognized under one division called the "Oriental." The Oriental—in shorthair—has championship status in all associations.

Persian. Persians are sweet, placid, quiet, and affectionate companions. Although they are known as the most sedentary breed, they have their playful side as well. An Italian traveler is credited with bringing the first Persian cats to the European world in the 1600s. The Persian is famous for its long, thick, glossy fur, which can grow to eight inches in length. Persians, not surprisingly, are also known to require daily grooming. This breed is sometimes described as "a shoe box with legs" because of its compact, massive body style. Persians have small, rounded ears, large eyes, round head and face, and snub nose. Because of the snub nose, upper respiratory problems, weepy eyes, and malocclusions have been reported in Persians. In addition birthing difficulties have been attributed to the disparity between the Persian's broad head and comparatively narrow hips. For those who like a less extreme facial arrangement, TCA recognizes and promotes the Traditional or Doll Face Persian. The Persian has championship status in all associations.

Ragamuffin. Ragamuffins are docile, sweet, playful, and quiet. They easily learn to play fetch and are devoted to their human companions. The Ragamuffin is similar, but not identical, to the Ragdoll breed. The Ragamuffin became a separate breed in 1993 when Ragdoll breeders who had been members of the International Ragdoll Cat Association (IRCA) founded by the Ragdoll's creator, the late Ann Baker, broke away and renamed their cats in order to avoid violating the Ragdoll trademark established by Baker. The Ragamuffin comes in a variety of colors and patterns. This breed is currently accepted for championship in UFO and for registration in ACFA.

Ragdoll. Ragdolls are known for their exceptionally tolerant disposi-

tions and sweet, docile temperaments. They tend to go limp when picked up, like a child's ragdoll, and this trait earned the breed its name.

Surrounded by controversy and mystery, the Ragdoll is a large, color

(above)
The Persian's coat can grow up to eight inches long.

(below)
Persians are known for their sweet expressions.

pointed breed whose ancestry is uncertain. It originated in the United States in the 1960s and was probably created by crosses between longhaired domestic cats that possessed the gene for the pointed pattern, although a variety of stories exist regarding the breed's origins. The Ragdoll has medium-long, silky fur, a long, strong, powerful body, and large, brilliant blue eyes. Ragdolls come in four pointed colors: seal, chocolate, blue, and lilac, and three patterns: solid colorpoint, mitted, and bicolor. This breed has championship status in all associations except CFA.

Russian Blue. Russian Blues are gentle, well-behaved, quiet cats. They are usually reserved around strangers, but are playful, affectionate, and active with their own families. They make unobtrusive but ever-present companions. The breed is thought to have originated in the White Sea port town of Archangel (Arkhangelsk) in northern Russia. The first Russian Blues arrived in America in the early 1900s.

Long, lithe, and slender, the Russian Blue has wide-set, brilliant green eyes, large ears, and a slight upturn to the corners of the mouth that makes it appear to be smiling. Its fur is short, silky, plush, and so dense it stands out from the body. The guard hairs are tipped with silver, giving the cat a silvery sheen. The breed, which is accepted in one coat color only—solid blue—has championship status in all associations.

Scottish Fold. The Scottish Fold is affectionate, intelligent, sweet-tempered, soft-spoken, and adapts easily to new people and situations. Noted for its unique, button-down ears, the Fold was first discovered near Coupar Angus in Scotland in 1961. It was introduced to the United States nine years later. Its distinctive ears are produced by a dominant gene that affects the cartilage of the ears, causing them to fold forward and downward. The head is rounded, and the eyes are large and round, giving the cat an owl-like expression. The Fold gene has been associated with congenital skeletal deformities that can cause crippling, especially in cats with two fold-ear parents. Scottish Folds come in every color and pattern

Longhaired Scottish Fold. Also known as the Highland Fold, Scottish Fold Longhair, and Longhair Fold.

except those that indicate hybridization, such as the Siamese colors and pattern. The breed has championship status in all associations.

A longhaired version of the Scottish Fold was first officially recognized by TICA in 1987. The Scottish Fold Longhair is known by three different names. ACFA, AACE, and UFO refer to the breed as the Highland Fold. TICA, ACA, CCA, and CFA call it the Scottish Fold Longhair, and CFF refers to the breed as the Longhair Fold. AACE, ACFA, CCA, CFA, CFF, TICA, and UFO have accepted the Scottish Fold Longhair for championship.

Selkirk Rex. Selkirk Rex are fun-loving, playful, and affectionate. People oriented, they stay frisky and kittenish even as adults.

The first Selkirk Rex was found in an animal shelter in the United States in 1987 and is one of the newest rex breeds. It is a well-balanced cat with a medium to large rectangular body. Governed by a dominant gene, the Selkirk's coat is curly, soft, and plush. The curl is more pronounced around the neck and tail, and even the whiskers are curly, which gives the face a whimsical appearance. The Selkirk comes in both shorthair and longhair varieties. In the longhaired variety, the Selkirk's coat is arranged in loose, individual curls. All colors are accepted including pointed colors. The breed has provisional status in CFA, new-breed-and-color status in ACFA and CCA, and championship status in the ACA, TICA, and UFO.

Siamese. Determinedly social, Siamese cats crave attention. They are vocal, demanding, and devoted to their owners. Their voices often possess a distinctive rasp. They are active and intelligent and can be taught a variety of tricks. Unfortunately, some members of this breed are troubled with endocardial fibroelastosis, a disease of the heart that can result in congestive heart failure and death.

The Siamese is one of the oldest cat breeds and is arguably the best-known breed on the planet. The Siamese is described and depicted in the *Cat-Book Poems*, a manuscript written in the city of Ayudha, Siam, sometime between 1350 and 1767. The breed is known for its extremely svelte, lithe body, large

The Siamese is the most popular shorthaired purebred.

pointed ears, brilliant blue eyes, and distinctive pattern in which the cat's points (mask, ears, tail, legs, and feet) are a darker color than the rest of its body. The Siamese was recognized originally during the late 19th century in seal, then in blue (1934), chocolate (1952), and lilac (1955). Some associations accept additional colors and patterns in the Siamese breed, but in CFA such cats are classified as a separate breed called Colorpoint Shorthairs. TCA recognizes and promotes the Traditional Siamese (also called the Old Style or Applehead), which possesses a more moderate body style and head type. The Siamese has championship status in all associations.

Siberian. Siberians are devoted, docile, playful, affectionate, intelligent cats. One of the largest breeds, the Siberian first arrived in the United States in 1990, but has existed in its Russian homeland for hundreds of years. It is a large, powerfully built cat with a rounded barrel-shaped torso, large ears, and large, expressive eyes. Despite its size (up to 16 lbs.), it is extremely agile and is a great jumper. The Siberian possesses a long, thick coat with a full ruff and an undercoat that becomes thicker in cold weather. Brown tabby is the most common color, but all colors and patterns except the pointed varieties are recognized. The breed has championship status with AACE, ACA, CFF, UFO, NCFA and TICA, and new-breed-and-color status in ACFA.

Singapura. Singapuras are active, affectionate, and quiet. They love being the center of attention. They're curious, people oriented, and remain playful well into adulthood. Noted in the *Guinness Book of World Records* as the smallest breed of domestic cat, the Singapura allegedly was brought to America from Singapore in the early 1970s, although controversy exists about its origins, and some critics claim it is not a natural breed at all. The Singapura is a small, moderately stocky, muscular cat with large, expressive eyes and large, deep-cupped ears. The cat's coat is short and is ticked like the Abyssinian's. Each hair has alternating bands of dark brown (called sepia) and warm, old-ivory color. The muzzle, chin, chest, and stomach are the color of unbleached muslin. Some breeders claim the Singapura is prone to the renal disease amyloidosis. The breed has championship status in all associations.

Snowshoe. Like the Siamese, Snowshoes never lack topics of conversation. They do, however, lack the Siamese rasp that some cat lovers find annoying. Snowshoes are affectionate, devoted to their owners, and don't like to be left alone.

A pointed-pattern breed with pure white boots, the Snowshoe was developed in the United States in the late 1960s from crosses between Sealpoint Siamese and bicolor American Shorthairs. This shorthaired, medium-sized cat incorporates the heftiness of the

American Shorthair and the body length of the Siamese. The combination of moderate body style, pointed pattern, and areas of white make this breed stand out. The face often bears an inverted "V" pattern. Accepted colors are blue and seal. The eyes are brilliant blue. The breed has championship status in AACE, ACFA, CFF, TICA, and UFO, and new-breed-and-color status in ACA.

Somali. The Somali has an active, curious and high-spirited personality almost identical to that of its close relative, the Abyssinian. Somalis are determined cats. Once they get an idea in their heads, it's hard to dissuade them.

Longhaired kittens began appearing in Abyssinian litters in the early 1900s, but it wasn't until the 1960s that breeders began efforts to develop these cats into a distinct breed. The Somali shares the ticked coat pattern, lithe, graceful body, large, alert ears, and almond-shaped, expressive eyes of the Abyssinian. The only genetic difference between the two breeds is the Somali's semilong coat, which is soft and extremely fine. The tail displays a full brush. The breed comes in four ticked colors: ruddy, red, blue, and fawn. Although generally healthy, the Somali is known to be susceptible to gingivitis and the renal disease amyloidosis. The breed has championship status in all associations.

Sphynx. Sphynxes are lively, agile, and energetic. Devoted and loyal, they demand unconditional love from their owners and tend to shadow their owners' movements. The only breed of domestic cat that is virtually hairless, the Sphynx is guaranteed to raise eyebrows. The hairlessness is the result of a spontaneous recessive mutation that arose at various times and places from the domestic cat population in the United States and Canada. Not truly hairless, the Sphynx is covered with a fine down that is almost imperceptible to the eye and touch, giving the skin the texture of chamois and the feel of a hot water bottle. Despite the lack of fur, Sphynxes must be bathed regularly to remove their natural skin oils. They come in all colors and patterns, which are evident on the fine down and the underlying skin. The breed has championship status in AACE, ACA, ACFA, CCA, TICA, and UFO.

Tonkinese. Tonkinese cats are active and agile. They crave—and return—affection and companionship, and have an unflagging enthusiasm for life. They love interactive toys such as their owner's fingers and the tails of their feline companions. Their voices are milder in tone than the Siamese. They do, however, believe in feline free speech.

The Tonkinese was developed in Canada in the early 1960s by a breeder who crossed a sable Burmese with a sealpoint Siamese. This cat strikes a balance between the extreme svelte and the cobby, compact body type. The Tonkinese possesses a sleek, soft, close-lying coat that has a lustrous sheen. The

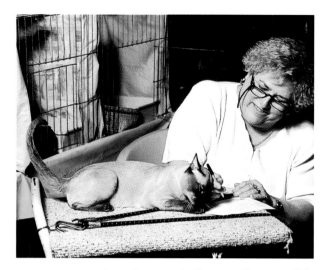

The Tonkinese is a cross between the Burmese and the Siamese.

semilong, fine, and silky, and seems to shimmer with every movement. Solid white is the most common color, but many colors and patterns are accepted. The breed has championship status in all associations.

Turkish Van. Vans are agile and intelligent and are famous for their action-packed temperaments. They are talkative and demanding of attention. Vans develop strong attachments to their human companions. They are inclined to pick out one or two people in the household—usually the ones that tend to them initially—and bond with them forever.

The Turkish Van originated in the Lake Van region of Turkey. Native ornaments dating as far back as 5000 B.C. depict cats that look remarkably like the Turkish Van. In 1955 two British citizens were given two Van kittens while touring Turkey, and this started the Van on the road to acceptance as a breed in Britain and North America. The Van is a solidly built, semilonghaired cat that takes three to five years to reach full maturity. It has a unique water repelling, cashmerelike coat. The Van possesses the classic "Van" pattern—it has a mainly white body with colored markings preferably restricted to the head and tail. Some Vans have a color patch between the shoulder blades called the "Mark of Allah," which is considered good luck in Moslem countries. The breed has championship status in AACE, ACFA, CFA, TICA, and UFO, and experimental status in CFF.

breed comes in three patterns: solid, like the Burmese, pointed, like the Siamese, and mink, a combination of the two. In the mink pattern, the shading from point color to body color is subtle and not as sharply defined as in the pointed pattern. All Tonkinese have deep, brilliant aquamarine eyes. The breed has championship status in all associations, but is not accepted in all colors by every association.

Turkish Angora. Angoras are highly intelligent and like to have control over their surroundings. They dislike being held and will only tolerate cuddling for a few minutes. They do, however, form strong, loving bonds with their human companions.

One of the oldest breeds, the Turkish Angora has lived in Turkey and the surrounding areas for centuries. It is an extraordinarily graceful cat with a long, willowy body, large, pointed ears and large, expressive, almond-shaped eyes. The coat is

Chapter 4
Selecting a Show Cat

One cat just leads to another.

—*Ernest Hemingway*

Cat breeders—indeed, animal breeders of all types—do not enjoy untarnished reputations these days. The emergence of the animal rights movement in the 1980s, the publication of several widely distributed magazine articles (see Useful Addresses and Literature, page 125) that took aim at the American Kennel Club and the genetic deficiencies that plague purebred dogs, and several highly visible television shows on the same topic have brought to light information that many breeders have long ignored, but that many people who purchased purebred animals know well: A pedigree and a registration certificate do not guarantee good health or sound temperament. Nor do they guarantee that the names on the pedigree are really the names of an animal's predecessors. There is also no guarantee that someone is in fact a reputable breeder. However, you can determine some degree of reputability by simply looking for high standards and other qualities explained in this chapter.

About Reputable Breeders

Unfortunately no intelligence or integrity tests are required of persons who take it upon themselves to breed and to sell cats. The person who advertises cats for sale may be a conscientious, compassionate individual motivated solely by the love of her chosen breed and the desire to contribute to its furtherance and perfection; or she might be an opportunist who would sell a kitten to anyone who pays with a certified check.

How a kitten is raised is also an important consideration. Kittens raised away from human contact won't be well-socialized.

The Persian is the most popular pure-bred breed by a substantial margin.

You don't need to see criminal neglect to tell the difference between the unscrupulous and the reputable breeder. Indeed, reputability is directly proportional to some variables and inversely proportional to others. The more you can smell the presence of cats in a breeder's house, the less reputable she is likely to be. The more questions a breeder asks you about your reasons for wanting a cat, the more reputable she is likely to be. The more kittens a breeder has available, the less reputable she is likely to be. The more references from satisfied customers the breeder is able to supply, the more reputable she is likely to be. The fewer assurances the breeder requires about your willingness to return the cat if you cannot keep it for whatever reason, the

less reputable she is likely to be. The more cats you see in cages in a breeder's house, the less reputable she is likely to be.

Reputability is not solely a function of cleanliness. I knew a breeder once whose cattery floor was so spotless you could eat off it. That was largely because her cats never did. Indeed, they seldom got out of their cages unless they were going to the vet's, the grooming table, or a show. This breeder believed "it's not in a cat's nature to be bored." Apparently she believed it wasn't in a cat's nature to enjoy play or exercise either.

Although temperament and good health are heritable to some degree, the way a kitten is raised is more important in shaping its personality and in determining its state of health. Kittens that are not handled often enough between the ages of three and 14 weeks are less likely to develop into well-adjusted family members than are kittens that receive frequent handling and attention during that interval. Therefore, it is well to ask how many litters a breeder produces each year and how many other litters she was raising when the kitten you are interested in was growing up. A breeder who produces more than three or four litters a year—or who was raising two or three other litters while your kitten's litter was maturing—may not have had time to socialize every kitten in those litters properly. A breeder who raises one or two litters at a time has more opportunity to give each of those kittens the individual attention it deserves. In general, the smaller the cattery, the more user-friendly the kittens it will produce and the more healthy those kittens will be.

The Healthy Kitten

Before you—the prospective buyer—evaluate a kitten's show potential, you should evaluate its health. If a kitten isn't healthy, it isn't showable. Never buy a sickly kitten just because you think it's going to be a worldbeater as soon as it gets rid of that gunk in its nose and eyes.

A healthy kitten's eyes are bright, glistening, and clear. Its nose is cool and slightly damp. Its gums are neither pale nor inflamed. Its ears are

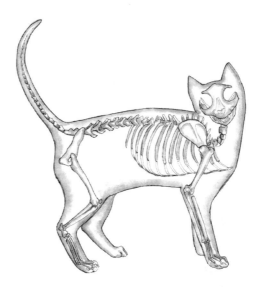

The 244 bones are classified into three groups according to shape: long, flat, and irregular. The radius and ulna in the front legs and the tibia and fibula in the hind legs are long bones. The scapula (shoulder blade) and the bones of the skull and face are flat bones. The metatarsals and metacarpals in the feet are irregular bones.

free of wax or dirt. Its body is soft and smooth, perhaps a little lean, but not skinny. Its coat is shiny and free of bald patches, scabs, or tiny specks of black dirt. The area around its tail is free of dirt or discoloration.

A kitten with teary eyes may be in poor health—especially if its nose is dry or if it feels warm. Inflamed gums may indicate gingivitis; a kitten with pale gums may be anemic. If its ears are waxy inside, that simply may be a sign of neglect; but if they exhibit caked-on dirt, the kitten may have ear mites. If a kitten's ribs are sticking out or if it is pot-bellied, it may be undernourished or it may have worms. A kitten with a dull looking coat or one dotted with

Like all mammals, cats possess voluntary and involuntary muscles. The latter, which are found in the alimentary canal, the urinary tract, and the cardiovascular and respiratory systems, are not controlled consciously. Voluntary muscles are secured to the skeleton by tendons. These "skeletal muscles," always arranged in pairs, work in cooperative opposition to each other.

their own cats, should start with the best quality female they can find. They also should remember that quality is not always proportionate to price and that registration papers merely indicate that a cat is eligible to be registered, not that it is good enough to be shown. Any registered cat can be entered in a show, but there is a qualitative difference between a cat that can be shown and a show cat. The former is costume jewelry, the latter is a genuine pearl—often of great price.

Novices are at an even greater disadvantage evaluating a cat's show potential than they are when gauging its general state of health. A runny eye is a runny eye to most observers, but eyes of the proper size, shape, and setting are more difficult for newcomers to identify, and the difficulty is compounded because kittens have yet to finish maturing.

scabs, tiny specks of dirt, or bald spots may have ringworm, fungus, or fleas. A kitten with wet hindquarters may develop urine scalding; if they are dirty, he may have diarrhea. Both urine scalding and diarrhea are signs of potential poor health.

Finally, when you select a kitten, ask the breeder how that kitten behaves when being groomed, how frequently it has been groomed, and what sort of comb or brush the breeder uses with the kitten. If you go to the breeder's house to take delivery on your kitten, ask for a grooming demonstration.

Fanciers interested in buying a show cat, and in eventually breeding

That is why a journey of hundreds of dollars (or more) must begin with a few simple steps: visit shows, talk to breeders, watch classes being judged, and learn what winning cats look like. Talk to judges when they have finished judging and ask them to recommend one or two breeders. If possible, visit several breeders who are willing to spend an afternoon or evening showing their cats at home.

Most important, study the breed standard of any breed in which you have an interest. Take a copy of the standard along when you go to look at kittens, and ask breeders to point

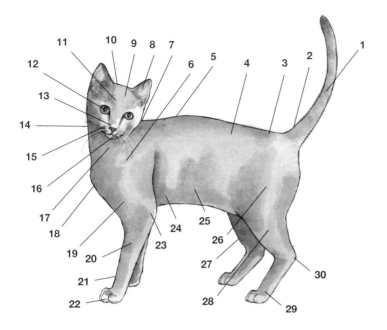

The external
anatomy of
the cat.
1. Tail
2. Base of tail
3. Rump
4. Back
5. Withers
6. Shoulder
7. Nape
8. Ear
9. Forehead
10. Crown
11. Occiput
12. Eye
13. Nose
14. Neck
15. Cheek
16. Whiskers
17. Throat
18. Chest
19. Upper arm
20. Lower arm
21. Metacarpus
22. Pad
23. Elbow
24. Rib cage
25. Belly
26. Upper thigh
27. Knee joint
28. Lower thigh
29. Metatarsus
30. Hock

out where a kitten or a cat meets the standard and where it does not. If the breeder does not object, take an experienced breeder along when you go to look at kittens.

Because breeders with the best available kittens will not always live within driving distance, you may have nothing more to base an informed decision on than a few pictures and the breeder's evaluation. If the pictures don't show the cat well, ask to see more. If you have any reason to doubt the breeder's word, find another breeder. In any case, ask the breeder to say, preferably in writing, where a kitten measures up to the standard and where it falls short. Breeders usually will not guarantee a kitten's performance in the show ring. As a Clint Eastwood character once said, "If you want a guarantee, buy a toaster." Nevertheless, a breeder should be willing to say whether a kitten looks like best-in-show material or top-ten finalist material. The breeder should give you a rough idea of how many shows the kitten will take, as an adult, to earn the titles the breeder thinks it is capable of earning in the various cat associations.

Anyone buying a show cat is also buying the constellation of genes that cat has inherited from its ancestors. The names and titles of the first four or five generations of ancestors are recorded on a cat's pedigree. Buyers should study a pedigree to see what titles the members of a kitten's family have won—especially its parents and grandparents, because the first two

Cat shows are good places to find reputable breeders.

Show Standards

Every cat in championship, alter, kitten, or provisional competition is judged according to a written standard for its breed. These standards are part blueprint because they describe the ideal specimen for the breed and part constitution because they can be revised by the members of a breed council. What's more, even though breed standards are theoretically precise enough to allow judges to evaluate cats objectively, they are still flexible enough to leave room for subjective differences in interpretation between judges of keen eye and good intention. Otherwise, the same few cats would win all the time, and most exhibitors would find other ways to spend the weekend and their money.

The first section of a breed standard quantifies a cat's virtues by assigning numerical values to them. The Scottish Fold standard in one association, for example, tells us that the Fold's head is worth 55 points and that of those 55 points ears are worth 25, head shape (including muzzle, neck, chin, and profile) is worth 15 points, and eyes are worth 15 points. The Fold's body is worth 40 points: 10 for the structure of the torso, legs, and paws, 20 for the tail, and 10 for the coat. The remaining 5 points are assigned to coat color and eye color.

Rather than getting bogged down in the minutiae of the standard—trying to decide, for example, whether a Fold has a 19-point or a 16-point

generations have the greatest impact on a kitten's development.

The most significant titles awarded in the show ring are grand champion, double, triple, and quadruple grand champion, and supreme grand champion. The more of these titles present in the first two or three generations of a kitten's pedigree, the better its ancestors have done in competition, and the better its chances, theoretically at least, of carrying on the family tradition.

Although some kittens never look anything but promising from an early age, the average youngster goes through several stages while it is growing up—from ugly duckling to swan and sometimes vice versa. Buyers should wait, therefore, until a potential show-quality kitten is five or six months old before buying it. A five- or six-month-old kitten is less subject to change without notice than is a younger kitten. Buyers are wise to wait until a show kitten has reached that age, and, perhaps, has been shown a time or two.

tail, you should use the standard as a guide to judge the order of importance of the cat's elements. That is what most judges will do, if they know the standard.

By rank-order logic, you begin evaluating a Fold by looking at her ears, tail, head, and eyes. Then you worry about coat quality and body type. Color you save for last. There's no point getting all excited about a Fold with perfect color, whatever that is, if her ears are barely folded. Remember, too, that a standard is as much a qualitative guide as it is a quantitative one. Judges don't stand in the ring going, "Let's see, this Fold has 22-point ears, a 13-point head, and 12-point eyes. Her tail's worth 19 points; her body structure's great, I'll give her all 10 points for that; her coat's a bit iffy, only worth 6 there, and her coat and eye color are good for 4 points. Now, how much are 22 and 13 and 12, plus 19, 10, 6, and 4? That's 84. Wait, no, that's 86. OK. This cat's an 86. Hmmm, what were the other cats in this class? Was that black-and-white one an 88 or an 85? Gosh, I'm hungry. When's lunch?"

If judges don't evaluate cats that way, neither should you. A cat is not the sum of its points, but what you should learn from the point section of a standard is the quality of the cat the judge is going to look at first. In our Fold example, that would be the ears and tail. Then the judge is going to look at a Fold's head and eyes, and because eyes are part of the head, she's probably going to look at the ears first, then the head, and then the tail, even though the tail is worth more individually than the head or the eyes are. Any faults in the ears or tail are going to do more damage to the cat's "score" than a muddy-colored coat is.

The other part of the standard, the narrative part, amplifies the point-score. The narrative section tells you, for example, that a Fold's ears should fold forward and downward and that small, tightly folded ears are preferred over a loose fold and large ear. The standard also tells you that a Fold's ears should be set in a caplike fashion to expose a rounded cranium and that the ear tips should be rounded.

Don't be fooled by the egalitarian sound of "are preferred over." If a standard tells you that some quality or other is preferred over some other quality, what it's really saying is that if the cat's going to do much

"Oh, I agree. Humans could never live up to such high standards."

winning, the quality in question better look the preferred way.

We need not quote nor discuss the rest of the Fold standard here. We do suggest again that you read the standard of every breed in which you are interested, and that you take a copy of the standard with you when you go shopping for kittens because the more a breeder is willing to apply the standard to the kittens she has available, the more reputable she is likely to be.

How to Evaluate a Pedigree

The ability to learn a new language without experiencing distress begins to fade around the age of five. It continues to diminish until we reach adulthood, whereupon our language-acquisition skills have deteriorated from the consistency of sponge to that of concrete. Perhaps this is why some people have difficulty understanding and interpreting pedigrees and putting them to good use. Though written in English, pedigrees are, to many breeders, manuscripts in a foreign, somewhat inscrutable tongue, fraught with their own vocabulary and rules of interpretation. Yet anyone who does not learn to speak pedigree fluently might just as well be pondering graffiti on a subway wall under a bad light if he hopes to use pedigrees as an aid to acquiring or later producing a good cat.

It's possible that the scholar who originated the phrase about reading between the lines was pouring over a stack of pedigrees when he did. Virtually all the information needed to understand a pedigree—what the cats on it look like, what their offspring and relatives are about, and what families they're most compatible with—is difficult to glean from the surface information on a standard three- or four-generation tome. What can be found there—a flurry of names, titles, and colors—merely constitutes a reasonable place to start reading; and as any student of language knows, reading ability begins with vocabulary.

Thus, elementary though it may seem, the first step to understanding a pedigree is to become familiar with all the names on it so that they mean something to you; because familiarity breeds good cats. In order to evaluate any pedigree, the novice exhibitor should study as many pedigrees as he can, and that study should be augmented by the study of cat association yearbooks; any publications, including those on the Internet, that include pictures of winning show cats, and especially the lists of sires and dams of grand champions published by some associations. These sources provide the pictures that are worth more than thousands of words on pedigrees, because they show you— albeit in a limited fashion—what winning cats look like and, possibly, what some of your prospective cat's ancestors looked like.

People who learn a second language, be it French, Pascal, or Pedigree, can be divided into two groups: those who can use the language and those who merely read it. Learning the basic Persian (or Siamese or whatever your chosen breed's) vocabulary, qualifies you for the readers' group; but to read with understanding and to progress into the users' group, you have to venture beyond vocabulary into the rules of grammar.

Because of grammatical rules (some would say despite them) there are many ways to express a notion gracefully. Likewise, there are many ways to breed a decent cat. Not all breeders observe precisely the same rules or employ the same style, but their compositions are generally guided by certain principles.

One is the principle of the proper match, or, to borrow a term from horse breeders, the good nick. Indeed, a horse breeder possessed of uncommon horse sense explained once that "too many people never discover the importance of learning what the compatible crosses are. Certain families simply don't cross well. Certain other families are golden crosses. The best way to find this out is by studying pedigrees intensely."

That breeder also said, "If you know something about the lines you want to work with, and if you know what other breeders have done with those lines, you can get a pretty good idea of what you're going to get from a particular breeding."

The study of pedigrees is an art, an ongoing discipline that's more process than product. The person who stops studying pedigrees can become as dated in a few years as the physician who stops reading medical journals.

A second principle of good breeding teaches that the close-up relatives on a pedigree are the most important: the sire and dam, grandsires and granddams. This is so because each generation contributes half as much to the genetic makeup of a cat as the preceding generation did. It is not wise, therefore, to put too many eggs in the basket of a great-great-grandparent perched high in the family tree. This cat provides 6.25 percent of a kitten's genetic makeup. An ancestor that far removed from center stage would have to leapfrog three generations of extras in order to play a leading role in a successful, longrunning production. Yet many novice exhibitors buy a kitten with an otherwise undistinguished pedigree

When choosing a cat, be sure to spend some time playing with it. This will give you a good idea of the cat's temperament.

because its great-great-grandfather was a national award winner.

Though the initial generations on a pedigree are the most influential, it is not always the first to whom the new is tied. Many times you will see a top-winning cat that has two rather ordinary looking parents, but when you see the four grandparents, you begin to salivate.

This phenomenon is known as the skip-a-generation rule. If you keep this rule in mind, it should be easy to answer the following question: Which is more valuable in a breeding program, a mediocre cat from a good pedigree or a good cat from a mediocre one? Such is the influence of the skip-a-generation rule that many wise breeders contend, "You're almost always breeding grandparents when you breed a pair of cats." For that reason, they'll tell you, even a great cat from a mediocre pedigree isn't going to throw much of anything good because "there's nothing good behind it to throw."

The mediocre pedigree usually gives itself away in the second and third generations. Both cats in the first generation could be breeders rather than show cats and the pedigree might well be worth the price of the cat, but if the grandparents and great-grandparents are not so great either, chances are the pedigree isn't worth the paper it's written on, no matter how good the fourth and fifth generations look.

The skip-a-generation rule is an equal-opportunity institution: It applies to bad traits as well as good. This tendency can sometimes be turned to a person's advantage. A stud cat with a conformation fault might seldom pass that fault on if one of his parents (or preferably both) is especially good in that regard.

The importance of the distaff contribution to a pedigree is one rule of breeding grammar that is frequently overlooked. Unfortunately, a homely granddam that you didn't pay much attention to because you were dazzled by the national winning male on the line above her on a pedigree can influence a kitten's type just as easily as the famous male will. There is no guarantee that he is any more genetically influential than she is. That's why a lot of breeders say they don't want to know about the sire in a proposed mating, they want to know about the dam's dam, for it's that second dam that will often put the bite to your plans.

While part of the knack of learning to speak Pedigree involves the ability to read between the lines, another part involves seeing the cats that are on the lines. "You should try to see as many of the cats in the first three generations of a pedigree as you can, even if it's only in pictures," one Persian breeder advises. And while you're at it, try to check out as many of the littermates of the cats that are on the pedigree. This is particularly important if a cat you are considering buying or breeding to is inbred. While the cat you're looking at may not have an extra ear, you

wouldn't want to be fooling with it if one of its littermates did.

Nearly 300 years ago William Penn remarked, "Men are generally more careful of the breed of their horses and dogs than of their children." Penn's observation is, perhaps, too cynical to apply to modern-day cat breeders, but the touchstone of good breeding has remained the same since Penn's day. The idea is to raise a kitten with a pedigree that's stronger than either of its parents' taken alone—a pedigree that will do the most to advance a breeder toward his goal.

Chapter 5
The Paper Trail

Education is what you get from reading the fine print. Experience is what you get from not reading it.

—Unknown

People make contracts when they buy groceries at the supermarket, food in a restaurant, or tickets at a theater. A checking account is the subject of a contract with a bank; and the purchase of a cat or kitten is accomplished by means of a contract with a breeder.

Contracts

For all their ubiquity, the nice thing about contracts is, you don't need a lawyer—or even a notary—to make one. Yet even though you can get by without a lawyer, you cannot get around the obligation of playing by the rules of law when you enter into a contract. All contracts are subject to review in court, and the court can be a fussy proofreader.

The laws governing contracts today stipulate that a contract consists of an offer, an acceptance, and a consideration between parties who have the legal capacity to make a contract. In most states persons who are sane, sober, and old enough can enter into contracts. Persons who are incompetent, not sober, or too young to understand the effects of a contract cannot. More precisely, they can make a contract, but they aren't necessarily bound by its provisions.

A valid contract begins with an offer, defined in part by one legal scholar as "a manifestation of assent to enter into a bargain." In addition to being indisputably clear, an offer must contain the names of the parties to the proposed contract, the subject matter of the contract, the price, and the time limit in which the contract must be performed.

One thing an offer does not have to contain is writing. Despite the wisdom of movie maker Samuel Goldwyn's observation, "a verbal contract isn't worth the paper it's written on," the late Melvin Belli, a well known San Francisco attorney, points out that "an oral contract is just as good as a written [one]." It's just not as easy to enforce if the parties disagree about what they agreed on. In order to protect your interests as well as your friendships, be sure that any contract you make is conveyed in writing.

Because an offer depends on the expression of consent by the person to whom the offer was made (the offeree), a contract must also contain an acceptance: an it's-a-deal response from the offeree. This response can be verbal, written, or a profound inclination of the head.

At the heart of every contract is the consideration: something either given or promised in exchange for a promise. In breeders' contracts the something either given or promised is a cat, kitten, or stud service, and the promise given in exchange is usually the promise to send money or a *kittenback.* Kittenback means that in exchange for the cat or the stud service, the seller will receive a kitten from the first litter in lieu of money. (A kittenback is a variable-worth form of currency, as evidenced by the abundant forms of the expression, "I'll let you have this female for $___.__ or a kittenback.")

These are the ties that bind offerer and offeree in a contract, but there is another law that cat breeders must consider: the law promulgated by that esteemed legal scholar Murphy, who opined that if anything can possibly go wrong, it will. Therefore, we need to cross-examine the elements of a contract with an eye toward the possibilities for misfortune that lurk within each.

There isn't too much that can go wrong in the neighborhood of legal capacity. The prospective cat buyer can generally tell (or inquire) if a person offering to sell a cat is daft, drunk, or underage. Moreover, most cat contracts are made between principals, not agents, so there is seldom any need to mess with Mr. or Ms. In-between. In the rare instance that you are approached by an agent offering to sell you a cat, ask to see a copy of the agent's authority in writing, and ask the agent to state, again in writing, whether or not the person she represents has put any price limitations or other conditions on the terms of the sale.

Once we paddle out from the shore of contractual authority into the tides of offers, acceptances, and revocations, the legal waters become deeper and more troublesome. Suppose, for example, a breeder's cat makes only one final at a show, and that breeder says to you, "If somebody offered me $15 for this lousy cat, I'd take it." Don't bother to reach for your checkbook. Offers made in jest are not binding.

Kittens are always captivating, but choose carefully and read the contract before you agree to buy. The cat will likely be with you for many years.

Offers that contain mistakes are. So if a breeder who means to set the price of a kitten at $750 types $700 on the contract instead, that contract is legally binding.

Although an offer "confers on the offeree the power to create a contract," the offerer has the power to revoke an offer before it is accepted. If, for instance, someone offers to sell you a cat for $500 and gives you a week to think about it, that person can revoke the offer, and that revocation need not be written or verbal. Action can speak louder than words if those actions are inconsistent with an intention to make a contract.

Keep in mind, however, that unlike an acceptance, which is effective upon dispatch (as soon as the offeree mails money and an acceptance letter), a revocation becomes effective only upon receipt. Thus, if you have mailed a breeder the money for a kitten and two days later you get a letter saying the kitten is no longer for sale, you are entitled to the kitten, as long as you can prove you mailed the check before you received the notice that the kitten was no longer for sale. The easiest way to prove this is by sending the money by registered mail so you will have a receipt to prove when you mailed your acceptance.

Remember, too, that once a breeder accepts a deposit on a cat or kitten, that breeder cannot revoke the offer to sell that animal. Breeders will often do this if a cat or kitten turns into a worldbeater between the time you agreed to buy it and the time the breeder calls you and offers to sell you another cat or kitten in its place. You do not have to accept that offer. That cat or kitten is yours, no matter how desperately the breeder wants to keep it.

The consideration—the *raison d'etre* of every contract—is perhaps its least troublesome area, especially in cat contracts, where the seller's consideration is a kitten, cat, or stud service and the buyer's consideration is money or a kittenback. The key to understanding considerations is remembering that they are two-way streets. If only one party makes a consideration, that's a gift; and gifts, like offers made in jest, are not binding.

A corollary of Murphy's Law of Contracts dictates that the possibility of litigation is directly proportional to the number of strings attached to a contract, and breeder's contracts, unfortunately, often come equipped with more strings than the Boston Pops. Some of those strings would be out of tune in a legal composition.

Many contracts, for example, specify that a kitten offered for sale cannot be declawed. But, says one lawyer, "A person could run into problems trying to enforce that contract. What if the cat is destroying furniture in its new home and the owners have tried every possible method of getting it to stop?" Or what if the sellers live a thousand miles away from the cat's owners? How is the former going to know if the latter are abiding by a questionable clause in a contract?

Another source of difficulty is the buy-back clause, in which the seller specifies that she must be given first option of buying a cat back at the original price if the buyer decides to sell or to place it. The part about the right of first refusal is fine, but the original-price part isn't. By insisting on buying a cat back at the original price, the seller is depriving the buyer of the right to benefit from the time and money he puts into the cat and from any increase in the cat's value because of its breeding or show-ring achievements.

The going rate for the cat is often determined by what someone else is willing to pay for it. If you buy a kitten for $750 and two years later someone makes you a legitimate offer of $1,000 for it, that's the going rate, and that's the rate the breeder should have to pay if she has first option to buy the kitten back because you cannot keep it.

Breeders load their contracts with hordes of provisions in hopes of protecting their kittens as much as possible. Such intentions are laudable, but they are not always legal, especially when they are tantamount to taking the law into their own hands. Thus, contracts that specify the amount of penalty a buyer will have to pay for violating any part of that contract are not likely to be enforceable. Nor is the part of a contract enforceable that says that any trial arising as a result of the buyer's breaching the contract will occur in the seller's home state and that the buyer will be responsible for court costs and attorneys' fees. These are matters for a court to decide. What's more, in interstate cases a federal court automatically has jurisdiction. The federal court may decide to change the venue to another state, but a breeder can't make that determination.

Despite the need for caution and realistic expectations in drawing up a contract, a breeder does have certain rights. Breeders can enforce a contract that specifies that the buyer of a kitten cannot sell the kitten—or any of its future offspring—to a pet shop, animal dealer, or research lab. The same would not apply if a specific individual was named as someone to whom the buyer of a kitten could never sell its offspring. A breeder can also enforce a stipulation that says a kitten cannot be used for breeding or showing.

While they try to exert some control over the fates of the kittens they sell, breeders are often particularly demanding about the use of whole males, and some contracts specify that the buyer of a male can use a male only with his own females and that he must have owned a female for a certain length of time before a breeding takes place. This is fine, says an attorney, "if the breeder says he wants to preserve the status of his bloodlines and that by allowing the buyer to breed to outside females he would be disseminating those lines. Therefore, he's putting in the no-outside-females stipulation. That would probably stand up. I also think the time-period stipulation would hold as long as it was reasonable."

Selecting a show cat requires careful consideration. Remember that you are buying a companion as well.

And what if a stud you buy turns out to be a dud? According to Belli, the buyer can get a refund. "Suppose Molly sells you a champion male show dog for $1,000, and you have plans to breed it," wrote Belli. "After several months of failure your vet tells you the dog is sterile. If Molly knew why you were buying the dog but didn't know it was sterile, you can rescind the contract based on your mutual mistake and get your money back." (If Molly knew the dog was sterile, "you have a good case for fraud.")

Contracts for stud service present their own set of potential difficulties. In general, a breeder can require that a female arrives with favorable results on every appropriate test known to veterinary science, and the breeder can also reserve the right to return the female if she does not think the cat is in good health. A breeder cannot, however, disclaim all responsibility for any loss or injury that occurs while the cat is in her possession. If the cat has a heart attack, the breeder's obviously not liable; but if she leaves a window open in her cattery and the cat runs off into the woods, the breeder most likely is liable. And if the cat returns pregnant, the breeder might also be liable for the difference between what those kittens and a pedigreed litter are worth. Other stud service considerations such as live-kitten guarantees, return services if the breeding doesn't take, boarding fees, and responsibility for shipping costs should all be spelled out clearly in the contract.

Contracts once signed, though binding, are not carved in stone. They can be modified in writing or verbally, even if they contain a clause that states they cannot be modified verbally. But if a contract is to be modified, there must be an additional consideration. For example, if someone offers to sell you a cat for $1,000 and you accept, and a month later he calls and says the cat has improved and he needs to get $1,250 for it, you are not bound to accept the new price—though you are still bound to honor the contract. And even if you say OK to the new price, you aren't bound by that acceptance because the seller didn't offer any additional consideration that justified the additional money. What the seller did, in effect, was accept the promise of a gift, and gift promises are not binding.

Buyers should read a contract meticulously before signing it because contracts are legally binding once they have been signed by both parties. If a contract contains any bizarre or intrusive stipulations that buyers do not understand or do not wish to accept, such as a stipulation saying that the breeder of the cat is entitled to come by and visit that cat on occasion, they should discuss these issues with the breeder before signing.

The present discussion attempts to present the first rather than the last word on contracts. It is not intended as legal advice. What's more, because contract law varies from one state to another, we sug-gest you consult an attorney before entering into a contract if you have any questions about its provisions. And if you should get into a dispute over a contract, don't take the law into your own hands, you take 'em to court.

Papers and Health Certificates

The most important documents that accompany a kitten to its new home are its health records. The records should be issued by the kitten's veterinarian and should list the dates that kitten was examined, the vaccinations it received, and the veterinarian's comments about the general state of the kitten's health. A

This exhibitor is filling out a claim for her cat's championship status. Attention to detail is important when providing information to the cat associations.

kitten should not leave home without these records, and a buyer should not accept a kitten without them. Some breeders, especially those that produce a large volume of kittens, like to save money by giving vaccinations themselves. There is nothing illegal about this, yet there is more to immunizing a kitten than drawing vaccine into a syringe and pushing the plunger. Breeders are not capable of examining kittens as thoroughly as a veterinarian can before administering vaccinations. This examination is important because vaccine given to a sick kitten does more harm than good. Thus, a kitten should be seen by a veterinarian at least once before it is sold, and that visit should occur before the kitten's first vaccination. Of course, the kitten should return to the vet for a health check before it is shipped to its new owner.

Registering Your Cat

In addition to the pedigree, new owners of a show cat will receive papers with the cat. These papers usually consist of a registration slip that the new owners fill out and send, along with the appropriate registration fee to the administrative office of the association in which that kitten's litter has been registered. The association then returns a certificate of ownership to the new owners.

A person buying a cat or kitten that already has been registered by its breeder will receive an owner's certificate. There is a transfer-of-ownership section on the back of the certificate that must be signed by the breeder and the new owner. Once the required signatures are in place, the new owner mails the certificate, with the appropriate transfer fee, to the administrative office of the association in which the cat has been registered. The association will send back a new, amended certificate of ownership to the new owner(s).

Fanciers who are interested in registering their cats in more than one association should contact the other association(s) in which they want to register the kitten and request the necessary forms. Usually the additional associations will want to see a copy of the kitten's pedigree and photocopied proof that the kitten has been registered in another association.

The American Association of Cat Enthusiasts, for example, will register a cat already registered in another association if the cat's owner fills out an official AACE registration form, listing four generations of the cat's ancestors. In addition the cat's owner must send a copy of the cat's registration from another recognized association. The owner's social security number or the number of one of the owners must be listed in the required location on the application to facilitate computer record keeping and to safeguard the owner's information.

Registering a Cattery Name

A cattery name, like that of a product, corporation, or team, should be snappy, easily remembered, and distinctive. In the following fictional example—any resemblance to catteries living or dead is purely coincidental—cattery names appear as both prefix and suffix: Hairball's Million Dollar Baby of Sycophant. The first cattery name, Hairball, identifies the cattery that bred the cat. The second cattery name, Sycophant, identifies the current owner of the cat, except in those cases in which a cat has been sold a second time and the current owner did not bother to substitute his cattery name for that of the previous owner. "Million Dollar Baby," of course, is the cat's registered name. More likely than not, that is not what the cat is called around the house. That name, referred to as a cat's "call name," is usually a shortened form of the registered name, "Milly," for example.

Cattery name registration forms are available from each of the cat associations. These forms can be obtained by writing to the association or, in some cases, by downloading them from the association's Website. No matter how a cattery name registration form is obtained, several rules must be observed to register a cattery name. To wit, a cattery name must be unique (i.e., it cannot be a name or a too-close-for-comfort variation of a name already registered by another cat fancier). The rules for cattery names—whether they may be one word or more, whether they may contain punctuation marks, and so on—vary from one association to another.

Cattery names are permanent records of the associations with which they are registered. Exhibitors may not change a cattery name once it has been recorded and approved, but they may register as many cattery names as they wish. When a cat fancier applies for a cattery name, he is usually asked to provide a second and a third choice in case the first name is already taken.

A person with a registered cattery name is allowed to use that name as a prefix only if he is the breeder of a cat. The person buying the cat may add his cattery name as a suffix to a

A distinctive cattery name and a flair for decorating will help you promote your cattery.

Hundreds of shows are held each year in the United States and Canada.

cat's name. And If the new owner is the third or subsequent owner of a cat, he may remove a previous owner's cattery name as a suffix and substitute his own name. (Associations generally restrict the number of letters permitted in a cat's name.

Therefore, if a cat has an unusually long registered name, there may not be room for a new owner to add his cattery name as a suffix to a cat's cattery name and registered name.) Fees for registering a cattery name vary among associations.

Chapter 6

Where the Shows Are

The cat is, above all things, a
dramatist.

—*Margaret Benson*

Every weekend of the year, with
the exception of those years
when Christmas falls on a Saturday
or Sunday, numerous cat shows are
held throughout the United States.
Unless you devoutly avoid newspapers and television news shows you
have probably seen an advertisement for a cat show or a 30-second
report on a show that was held in
your area. Indeed, you may have
even seen a show televised on one
of the cable channels.

How to Find a Cat Show

Magazines and Newspapers

Cat magazines list hundreds of
shows held each year in the United
States and Canada. If there isn't a
cat magazine on the rack at a news-
stand or supermarket near you, call
one of their subscription depart-
ments (see Useful Addresses and
Literature, page 125) and ask to buy

the latest issue. Newspapers, too,
may contain notices for cat shows in
the "Pets" section of the classified
ads or in the notices of coming
events in the "Living," "Lifestyle," or
"Weekend" sections.

Cat Associations

The various cat registering bodies
in North America that license shows
(see page 125) may also be helpful
in this regard. If you have an Internet
service provider, fire up your Web
browser and punch in the Web
address of an association. You may
find a list of upcoming shows there.
You may also find a list of cat clubs.
If you do not have an Internet service provider or if you are interested
in an association that is not com-
puter-friendly yet, call that association and request a list of shows.

The Entry Form and the Show Flyer

Once you have obtained information about a show (no matter where
you obtained it), call or write to the
entry clerk for that event to request a
show flyer and an entry form. The

The wait between shows can be long, so bring along something to read. Your favorite cat magazine or It's Showtime! *would be appropriate choices.*

flyer provides the show hall location, the time the show begins, and the hours when exhibitors can check in their cats. The flyer also discloses whether the show committee will provide litter, litter pans, and cat food for all entries, and what special trophies or prizes will be awarded at the show. Flyers announce the entry fee, the date on which the club will

To prevent the spread of disease, each cage in the show ring is cleaned before a new group of cats is brought in. All the same, be sure your cat's vaccinations are up to date before entering a show.

stop taking entries, and the judges who will officiate at the show. Flyers remind exhibitors that all household pet entries must be neutered or spayed, that all cats' inoculations should be up to date, that cats from catteries where infectious illness has occurred during the last 21 days are not allowed in the show hall, and, if local law requires, that exhibitors must bring along proof that their cats have been vaccinated against rabies.

Filling out the entry form, while not as taxing as filling out the 1040 long form and several of its attendant schedules, still requires some attention to details. On the entry form an exhibitor provides the name of the cat being shown, its owner's name, the cat's breed, color, registration number, date of birth, parents, sex, and eye color, the class in which the cat will compete, the name of the person, if any, who will exhibit the cat for its owner, and the name of the person, if any, with whom an exhibitor would like to be benched. (Each cat entered in a show is "benched" or assigned to a cage where it remains when it is not being judged.) If an exhibitor has any questions about completing an entry form, entry clerks will answer them cheerfully before nine o'clock at night.

Once an entry form is completed, the exhibitor mails it with the appropriate fee to the entry clerk. Two-day shows cost $30 to $60, depending on the number of times a cat will be judged. One-day shows are proportionately less expensive.

The number of entries at a show usually is limited, and shows often reach their quota before the advertised closing date. To avoid being shut out, exhibitors should mail their entry forms at least two or three weeks prior to that date. If you enter a show and do not receive confirmation within two weeks after mailing your entry, phone the entry clerk to ask if the entry has been received.

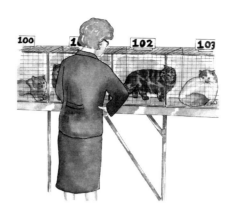

A show cat is evaluated according to the judge's subjective interpretation of a standard written to describe the ideal specimen of the breed.

Entry Confirmation

The entry confirmation contains a facsimile of the cat's listing in the show catalog, directions to the show hall, a list of motels near the hall, and other information. Exhibitors should proofread the confirmation to be sure all names are spelled correctly, the cat's registration number is accurate, and the cat has been entered in the correct class. Errors should be reported immediately to the entry clerk. After checking the confirmation, exhibitors should keep it in a safe, easy-to-recall place.

A Few Words About Judges

The men and women who judge at cat shows are thoroughly trained and, for the most part, well qualified in the art of cat judging. Cat show judges have demonstrated success at breeding cats and a knack for exhibiting them. Judges have served a lengthy apprenticeship in which they were on show committees in a number of capacities including show manager and entry clerk; they have acquired experience as ring clerks and master clerks; and they have demonstrated good moral character in the cat fancy.

A prospective judge must have a specified number of years of breeding experience (the exact number varies from one association to another) before they can apply to the judges program. Once accepted into the program, trainee judges must pass examinations on breed standards and show ring mechanics, and they must apprentice with certified instructors. The people who evaluate your cat may be school teachers, executives, blue collar workers, doctors, and lawyers during the week, but they are all masters of their second craft on show weekends, when they are privileged to meet the finest pedigreed cats in the land.

Cat Association Statistics

The following statistics are presented in order to give readers an estimate of the relative size of the cat registering bodies in North America. The existence of so many associations performing the same functions might at first seem like bureaucracy run amok, but we prefer to think of the associations as equivalent to the various kinds of races offered at a racetrack. Not every horse is a stakes horse. Nor is every cat capable of winning in every association. Nevertheless, among them the associations offer levels of competition for cats of all kinds of merits and demerits. (In every case the statistics presented reflect an association's activity during the last year for which statistics were available at press time.)

The CFA licenses more shows each year than any other North American association.

The American Association of Cat Enthusiasts (AACE) licensed 19 shows during the 1996–97 show season. There were 16 clubs in AACE at that time. The association does not keep track of the number of new cats and kittens it registers each year.

The American Cat Association (ACA) licensed 17 shows in the 1996–97 show season. There were 42 ACA clubs at that time, and the association registered 3,000 new cats and kittens that year.

American Cat Fanciers Association (ACFA) licensed 67 shows in the 1996–97 show season. This association does not keep track of the number of new cats and kittens it registers each year.

The Canadian Cat Association (CCA) licensed nearly 50 shows in the 1996–97 show season. There were 20 clubs in CCA that year, and the association registered 3,886 new cats and kittens.

The Cat Fanciers' Association (CFA) licensed 429 shows during the 1996–97 show season. There were 650 CFA clubs that year, and the association registered 68,948 new cats and kittens.

The Cat Fanciers' Federation (CFF) licensed 28 shows during the 1996–1997 show season. There were 66 CFF clubs that year, and the association registered 1,309 new cats and kittens.

The International Cat Association (TICA) licensed 298 shows during the 1996–97 show season. There were 470 TICA clubs that year, and the association registered 13,016 new cats and kittens.

The United Feline Organization (UFO) licensed 35 shows in the 1996–97 show season. There were 30 clubs in UFO that year, in which the association registered between 75 and 100 litters and 1,465 individual cats.

The Traditional Cat Association and the National Cat Fanciers' Association were unable to provide the requested demographic information in time to have it included in this book.

Chapter 7
Keeping Score

For push of nose, for perseverance,
there is nothing to beat a cat.
—*Emily Carr*

C at fanciers live for the day they can put "GRC" in front of their cat's name. This, of course, is the standard abbreviation for Grand Champion. Generally, earning the title of Grand Champion or Grand

Most associations hold year end events where the best cats are honored with special awards and trophies.

Champion Alter (Grand Premier in CFA) means that your cat has competed in a number of shows and has been judged to be an outstanding example of its breed. Of course, winning is not as simple as it sounds. It takes an investment of time, money, and effort for your cat to earn titles and score points toward regional and national awards.

After a cat has met the requirements for a title, her owner is allowed to affix that title (usually in abbreviated form) in front of the cat's name on any certificate, advertisement, letter, or e-mail in which the cat's name is likely to appear.

In addition to titles, which are dispensed by each of the ten cat registering associations in North America, some owners seek regional or national awards for their cats. Like the various titles available, these awards are earned by defeating cats in competition. Unlike titles, which are granted after certain finite criteria have been met, the regional and national awards offered by various associations go to the cats accumulating the most points—and, usually, to the cat owners willing to drive or fly the most miles—during a show year. The cat fancy year, like other nonlunar years, follows it own schedule, beginning, in most cases, on May 1 and ending the following April 30. (The show year in the American Association of Cat Enthusiasts begins on November 1 and ends on October 31.)

Unfortunately, the ten cat registering associations in North America have not held a summit meeting yet to standardize their titles and scoring procedures, nor are they likely to in the near or distant future. Therefore, the novice exhibitor is obliged to learn the rules, regulations, scoring procedures, and names of the titles available in whatever association she wishes to have a cat compete. In the hope of making that learning process as painless as possible, we present in this chapter the requirements for earning the various titles and awards conferred by the ten cat registering associations in North America. Though we have worked diligently to be as accurate as possible in that regard, a few facts may have suffered in translation. A few other facts may be outdated. The diligent reader may also notice that the procedures for some associations are presented more fully than the procedures for other associations. This presentation in no way reflects any judgment of the relative merits of an association. It simply reflects the amount of information we were able to obtain from that association before this book went to print.

The Meaning of Titles

Pedigreed Cats

Why earn titles at all? Titles recognize excellence and are therefore very important in terms of validating a breeding program. For this reason, titled cats are critical to the success of a cattery. The goal of a reputable breeder's breeding program is not to produce as many kittens as possible. The goal is to produce *top quality* show cats—cats that meet the show standard and do well in competition. It's important to understand that instead of making money breeding cats, most reputable breeders sow thousands more than they reap. For most purebred cat breeders, breeding is a labor of love—a way of life

The big day has arrived! You've done all you can to prepare and now you'll see if Fluffy behaves herself in the show ring.

All associations have categories for household pets; some offer titles and year end awards, too.

rather than a money-making venture. Titles validate a breeder's hard work and confirm that the breeder is achieving his or her breeding goals. That's why cat shows are very competitive and exhibitors take the events so seriously.

Household Pets

The reasons for earning titles for a household pet are much the same as they are for obtaining a title on a purebred cat. People who seek to earn titles for their household pets do so because they love cats in general and their cats in particular—just as purebred owners do. Household pet owners want to show their cats off so the world can see what lovable, sweet, beautiful cats they are—just as purebred owners do. A title confirms the household pet owner's feelings for his cat, too, and showing in the household pet category is also fun. In fact, for many

people the cat fancy offers the best opportunity to socialize with like-minded cat lovers. Showing in household pet classes also provides an understanding of the showing process and, therefore, is a good place to begin a show career or to decide if you want to begin one.

Scoring Procedures

American Association of Cat Enthusiasts

Championship Competition

In the American Association of Cat Enthusiasts (AACE) championship competition is open to unaltered, pedigreed cats that are at least eight months old on the first day of the show. A cat does not have to be registered with AACE in order to be shown in a championship class as long as that cat has been registered with another cat association and the cat's owner has already applied for AACE registration for that cat. Owners can also make application for AACE registration for a cat at the show in which the cat will be competing.

The following nine titles can be earned in championship competition in AACE: champion, double champion, triple champion, quadruple champion, grand champion, double grand champion, triple grand champion, quadruple grand champion, and supreme grand champion. The requirements for those titles are:

Champion: four winner's ribbons, each one awarded by a different judge. *Champion* is the entry-level title in AACE as it is in the rest of the cat fancy. Cats working toward a championship in AACE begin their show careers in the open class, when they compete for winner's ribbons against other cats of their sex and breed. To earn a winner's ribbon a cat must finish first in his class.

Double champion: four additional winner's ribbons, each one awarded by a different judge. These may be the same judges that awarded the four winner's ribbons a cat earned to become a champion.

Triple champion: see double-champion requirements.

Quadruple champion: see double-champion requirements.

Grand champion: Cats that have earned the quadruple champion title advance to the champion class, where they compete for awards toward the grand champion title. In order to become a grand champion a cat must earn six top-ten final wins. (A *final win* is an award given to each of the cats selected by the judge as one of the ten best cats in show.) Three of those wins must be in allbreed rings, including a top-five allbreed placement. The other three may be specialty finals, including a top-three specialty placement. Any final wins a cat earns before becoming a champion, double champion, triple champion, or quadruple champion can be counted toward the requirements for its grand champion title.

Double grand champion: 30 grand-champion points earned by defeating other grand champions in competition. Cats that have earned a grand champion title compete in the grand champion class, where they can earn points and awards toward additional titles. Grand champion points are awarded on the following scale: 1 grand defeated = one point; two grands defeated = 2 points; three grands = 3 points; four grands = 4 points; five grands and up = 5 points.

Triple grand champion: same as for double grand champion.

Quadruple grand champion: same as for double grand champion.

Supreme grand champion: (1) 100 grand champion points earned after a cat has become a quadruple grand champion; and (2) a best-cat win in an allbreed ring.

Alter Competition

Alter competition in AACE is open to altered, pedigreed cats that are at least eight months old on the first day of the show. A cat does not have to be registered with AACE in order to be shown in an alter class as long as that cat has been registered with another cat association and the cat's owner has already applied for AACE registration. Cat owners can also apply for AACE registration for that cat at the show in which the cat is competing.

The following nine titles can be earned by altered, pedigreed cats in AACE: champion, double champion, triple champion, quadruple champion, grand champion, double grand champion, triple grand champion,

The show catalog lists all the entries and helps you keep track of the winners at the show.

quadruple grand champion, and supreme grand champion. The requirements for those titles are:

Champion: four winner's ribbons, each one awarded by a different judge. As it is in the classes for unaltered pedigreed cats, *champion* is the entry-level title sought by altered cats. Cats working to obtain that title compete for winner's ribbons in the open class against other members of their sex and breed. In order to earn a winner's ribbon a cat must win her class.

Double champion: four additional winner's ribbons, each one awarded by a different judge. These may be the same judges that awarded the four winner's ribbons a cat earned to become a champion.

Triple champion: see double-champion requirements.

Quadruple champion: see double-champion requirements.

Grand champion: Cats that have earned the quadruple champion title compete in the champion class for points toward the grand champion title. In order to become a grand champion a cat must earn six top-ten final wins (i.e., be selected as one of the ten best cats in show). Three of those wins must be in allbreed rings, including a top-five allbreed placement. The other three may be specialty finals, including a top-three specialty placement. Any finals wins a cat earns before becoming a champion, double champion, triple champion, or quadruple champion can be counted toward the requirements for its grand champion title.

Double grand champion: 30 grand-champion points earned by defeating other grand champions in competition. Cats that have earned a grand champion title compete in the grand champion class, where they can earn points and awards toward additional titles. Grand champion points are awarded on the following scale: 1 grand defeated = one point; two grands defeated = 2 points; three grands = 3 points; four grands = 4 points; five grands and up = 5 points.

Triple grand champion: same as for double grand champion.

Quadruple grand champion: same as for double grand champion.

Supreme grand champion: (1) 100 grand champion points earned after a cat has become a quadruple grand champion (2) a best cat win in an allbreed ring.

Nonchampionship Competition

AACE also offers classes for kittens, household pets, and breeds that have not been accepted yet for championship competition. (The latter compete in new-breed-or-color classes.) Cat associations do not award titles to kittens, but kittens do compete for finals awards at shows, as well as for regional and national awards. Household pets compete for titles and year-end awards in AACE, which offers the following titles for household pets: regal, double regal, triple regal, quadruple regal, imperial, double imperial, triple imperial, quadruple regal, and supe-

rior. Neither kittens nor household pets have to be registered in order to compete in an AACE show, but they must be registered if they are to be considered for titles or awards.

Regional and National Wins

Every time a cat makes a final in AACE he wins points toward a national or regional award. Those points are based on how high a cat places in finals or the number of cats the finals-making contestant defeated in the show. Cats earning the greatest number of points during a show season win the various post-season awards available from AACE. Cats must compete in a minimum of 24 rings in order to qualify for year-end awards. Kittens must compete in at least 16 rings.

Differently Abled Cats

Declawed cats and deaf cats can be shown in all classes in AACE shows. Blind cats and cats that have lost all or part of an ear, limb, or tail because of accident or injury cannot be shown.

American Cat Association

Championship Competition

In the American Cat Association (ACA) championship competition is open to unaltered, pedigreed cats that are at least eight months old on the first day of the show and are already registered with ACA. The following three titles can be earned in

championship competition in ACA: champion, grand champion, master grand champion. The requirements for those titles are as follows:

Champion: Six winner's ribbons from four different judges. Cats that have not yet earned their championships compete for winner's ribbons in the open class against other members of their sex and breed. A cat earns a winner's ribbon by winning her class. (In Hawaii, Alaska, and Japan—places in which the cat population is not as large as in the contiguous United States—a cat needs only two winner's ribbons from two different judges to become a champion.)

Grand champion: Cats that have earned the title of champion compete in the champion class, where they attempt to earn points and awards toward the grand champion title. The requirements for that title are: (1) ten top-five finals wins under five different judges. At least two of those wins must be in allbreed rings; (2) 100 grand championship points accumulated under at least five different judges, two of whom must be allbreed judges. (In Hawaii, Alaska, and Japan, a cat is required to earn only 50 grand championship points under two different judges.)

Master grand champion: Having completed the requirements for the grand champion title, a cat then competes in the grand champion class in order to win points and awards toward the master grand champion title. To achieve that title a cat must earn ten top-five final wins. Two of those wins must be earned in allbreed rings. In addition the cat must have been chosen best cat in show at least once in the open, champion, or grand champion class. Finally, the cat must have won a total of 200 master grand championship points under at least five different judges, two of whom must be officiating in allbreed rings. (In Hawaii, Alaska, and Japan, a cat needs only 100 master grand championship points under two different judges.)

Alter Competition

Alter competition in ACA is open to altered, pedigreed cats that are at least eight months old on the first day of the show and are already registered with ACA. The following three titles can be earned in alter competition in ACA: champion, grand champion, and master grand champion. The requirements for those titles are:

Champion: six winner's ribbons from four different judges. Altered cats that have not yet won their championships compete for winner's ribbons in the open class against other members of their sex and breed. A cat earns a winner's ribbon by winning his class. (In Hawaii, Alaska, and Japan a cat needs two winner's ribbons from two different judges.)

Grand champion: Cats that have earned the title of champion compete in the champion class, where they attempt to earn points and awards toward the grand champion title. The requirements for that title are: (1) four top-five finals wins under four different judges. One of these wins must be in an allbreed ring; (2) 50 grand championship points from four different judges, one of whom must be allbreed. (In Hawaii, Alaska, and Japan a cat needs 25 grand champion points from 2 different judges.)

Master grand champion: Having completed the requirements for the grand champion title in alter competition, a cat then competes in the grand champion class, where it attempts to earn points and awards toward the master grand champion title. In order to become a master grand champion, a cat must be selected at least ten times under five different judges, two of whom must be officiating in all-breed rings, as one of the top five cats in show. In addition the cat must earn 100 master grand championship points under at least four different judges, one of whom must be officiat-ing in an allbreed ring. The cat must also have been chosen best cat in show at least once in the open, champion, or grand champion class.

Nonchampionship Competition

ACA also offers classes for kittens and household pets. Kittens do not compete for titles, but they do compete for finals awards at shows, as well as for regional and national awards.

ACA was the first cat association to register household pets and to offer titles that household pets can earn in competition. Those titles are companion, grand companion, and master grand companion. Household pets are also eligible for year-end awards.

Regional and National Wins

Points are awarded to cats that win any of the top-five or top-ten final awards in championship or alter competition in ACA. These points are awarded on the basis of how high a cat places in finals. At the end of the show seasons, awards are presented to the owners of cats that have accumulated the greatest number of points in the various competitive categories.

Differently Abled Cats

Declawed cats cannot be shown in championship or alter classes in ACA. Neither can deaf cats, blind cats, or cats that have lost all or part of an ear, limb, or tail because of accident or injury be shown in either of these categories.

American Cat Fanciers Association

Championship Competition

Championship competition in the American Cat Fanciers Association (ACFA) is open to unaltered, pedigreed cats that are at least eight months old on the opening day of the show. In addition cats for whom a registration application has been received by the ACFA central office by the Friday prior to the first day of the show are eligible to compete in that show. Owners of those cats have 30 days to ask the central office to place their cats' numbers in the catalog and to award credit for any wins earned at that show.

The following eight titles can be earned in championship competition in ACFA: champion, double champion, triple champion, quadruple champion, grand champion, double grand champion, triple grand cham-

The judge is in charge of his ring. The ring clerk keeps records of wins; these forms must be signed by the judge.

pion, quadruple grand champion. The requirements for those titles are:

Champion: four winner's ribbons won under four different judges. (The ACFA board of directors may lower these requirements for cats whose owners live in remote areas. For example, a cat living in the back of beyond may be able to earn a championship with two winner's ribbons from ACFA shows and one winner's ribbon from another association's show.) Adult cats begin their careers in the open class, where they compete against other cats of the same sex, color, and breed for winner's ribbons. In order to earn a winner's ribbon, an open cat must win his class.

Double champion: four additional winner's ribbons won under four different judges. These may be the same judges that awarded the four winner's ribbons a cat earned to become a champion.

Triple champion: see requirements for double champion.

Quadruple champion: see requirements for double champion.

Grand champion: Having earned the title of quadruple champion, a cat must be selected best champion in show six times by six different judges. On at least two of those occasions that cat must be selected among the top five cats in show in an allbreed ring.

Double grand champion: having attained the title of grand champion a cat must earn 30 grand championship points by defeating other grand champion cats in competition. Grand champions compete in the grand champion class. If a cat wins a first place in that class, it wins one point for each grand champion cat it defeats up to a maximum of five points.

Triple grand champion: same as for double grand champion.

Quadruple grand champion: same as for double grand champion.

Alter Competition

Alter competition in ACFA is open to altered, pedigreed cats that are at least eight months old on the opening day of the show and are either registered with ACFA or have a registration number pending (i.e., their owners have applied for registration, and that application has been received by the ACFA central office by the Friday prior to the first day of the show). Owners of those cats have 30 days to ask the central office to place their cats' numbers in the catalog and to award credit for any wins earned at that show.

The following eight titles can be earned in alter competition in ACFA: champion, double champion, triple champion, quadruple champion, grand champion, double grand champion, triple grand champion, quadruple grand champion. The requirements for those titles are:

Champion: four winner's ribbons won under four different judges. As noted above, the ACFA board of directors may lower these requirements for cats whose owners live and compete in isolated areas. For example, a cat may be able to earn a championship with two winner's

ribbons from ACFA shows and one winner's ribbon from another association's show. Altered cats that have not yet earned their championships compete for winner's ribbons in the open class against other members of their sex and breed. A cat earns a winner's ribbon by winning his or her class.

Double champion: four additional winner's ribbons won under four different judges. These may be the same judges that awarded the four winner's ribbons a cat earned to become a champion.

Triple champion: same as for double champion.

Quadruple champion: same as for double champion.

Grand champion: Having earned the title of quadruple champion, a cat must be selected best champion in show six times by six different judges and on at least two of those occasions must be selected among the top five cats in show in an all-breed ring.

Double grand champion: After attaining the title of grand champion, a cat must earn 30 grand championship points by defeating other grand champion cats in competition. Grand champions compete in the grand champion class. If a cat wins a first place in that class, it wins one point for each grand champion cat it defeats up to a maximum of five points.

Triple grand champion: same as for double grand champion.

Quadruple grand champion: same as for double grand champion.

Nonchampionship Competition

ACFA offers competition for kittens, household pets, and breeds not yet accepted for championship competition. (The latter compete in new-breed-or-color classes.) ACFA does not award titles to kittens, but kittens do compete for finals awards at shows, as well as for regional and national awards. Household pets compete for titles and year-end awards in ACFA. Kittens and household pets do not have to be registered in order to compete in ACFA shows, but they must be registered in order for their owners to claim any awards their cats won at shows.

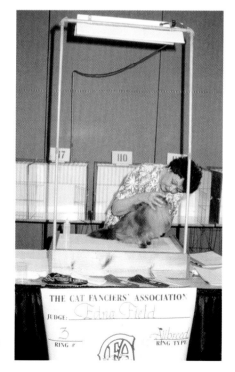

Each ring is marked by number, type (allbreed or specialty), and judge's name.

Regional and National Awards

Each time a cat is chosen among the top ten cats in show at an ACFA show or each time a cat is chosen best or second best of breed or best or second best of color, it receives points that count toward year-end awards in each of those categories. The central office keeps track of these points and presents regional and national awards to the cats that earned them.

Differently Abled Cats

Declawed cats and deaf cats can be shown in all ACFA classes. Blind cats cannot be shown. Cats that have lost all or part of a limb, ear, or tail because of accident or injury can be shown in household pet classes only.

Canadian Cat Association

Championship Competition

In the Canadian Cat Association (CCA) championship competition is open to unaltered, pedigreed cats that are at least eight months old on the first day of the show. A cat does not have to be registered in CCA in order to compete for winner's ribbons, but it may be shown only once without benefit of registration.

The following five titles can be earned in championship competition in CCA: champion, international champion, grand champion, international grand champion, and master grand champion. The requirements for those titles are:

Champion: four winner's ribbons awarded by at least three different judges. Adult cats begin their show careers in the open class, where they compete against other cats of the same sex and breed for winner's ribbons. In order to earn a winner's ribbon, an open cat must win her class.

Grand champion: To earn a grand championship a cat must acquire 150 grand champion points. Cats competing for grand champion points are entered in the champion class. If a cat is chosen best champion of its breed, it receives one grand champion point for every other champion of that breed that it defeated. In addition, the cat selected best champion in show earns one point for each champion defeated in the show. The second-best champion in show receives 90 percent of the points received by the best champion. Finally, the third-through tenth-best champions in show can earn grand points if they are selected among the top ten cats in show. The third-best champion receives 80 percent of the points won by the best champion. The fourth- through tenth-best champions receive points toward their grand championship on a downward progressing scale that ranges in increments of 10 percent—from 70 percent of the points won by the best champion in show to (for the fifth-best champion) 10 percent of the points won by the best cham-

pion in show (for the tenth-best champion).

Grand champion points must be won under at least three different judges, and on one of the occasions that a cat is chosen the best or second-best champion in show that cat must also be selected among the top five cats in show overall in either an allbreed or a specialty ring.

Master grand champion: To earn the title of master grand champion a cat must earn 125 master grand champion points under three different judges. Cats competing for these points are entered in the grand champion class. A cat receives one master grand champion point for every grand champion defeated in the show. The second best grand champion receives one point fewer than the best grand champion. The third- through tenth-best grand champions can also receive grand points if they are selected among the ten best cats in show. In that event the third-best champion receives two fewer points than the best grand champion, and so on through the tenth best champion, which receives nine fewer points than the best grand champion. In addition to earning 125 master grand champion points, a cat must earn a best-cat-in-show win.

Alter Competition

In CCA alter competition is open to altered, pedigreed cats that are at least eight months old on the first day of the show. A cat does not have to be registered in CCA in order to compete for winner's ribbons, but it may be shown only once without benefit of registration.

The following five titles can be earned in alter competition in CCA: premier, international premier, grand premier, international grand premier, and master grand premier. The requirements for those titles are:

Premier: four winner's ribbons awarded by at least three different judges. Cats that have not yet earned their premierships compete for winner's ribbon in the open class against other members of their breed and sex. In order to earn a winner's ribbon they must win their class.

Grand premier: 75 grand premier points. Cats competing for grand premier points are entered in the premier class. If a cat is selected best premier in show and is selected among the top ten cats in show, that cat earns one point for each premier defeated in the show. The second-best premier—if it finished among the top ten premiers in show—receives 90 percent of the points received by the best premier. Finally, the third-through tenth-best premiers can also earn grand premier points if they are selected among the top ten cats in show. In that event the third-best premier receives 80 percent of the points won by the best premier. The fourth-through tenth-best premiers receive points toward their grand premiership on a downward progressing scale that ranges in increments of ten percent—from 70 percent of the points won by the best premier in show (for the fifth-best premier) to 10 percent

of the points won by the best premier in show (for the tenth-best premier).

Grand premiership points must be won under at least three different judges, and on one of the occasions that a cat is chosen the best or second- through tenth-best premier in show that cat must also be selected among the top five cats in show overall in either an allbreed or a specialty ring.

Master grand premier: To earn the title of master grand premier a cat must earn 35 master grand premier points. Cats competing for these points are entered in the grand premier class. A cat receives one master grand premier point for every grand premier defeated in the show. The second best grand premier receives one point fewer than the best grand premier. The third-through tenth-best grand premiers can also win master grand premier points if they are selected among the top ten cats in show. In that event, the third-best grand premier receives two fewer points than the best grand premier, and so on through the tenth best premier, which receives nine fewer points than the best grand premier. In addition to earning 125 master grand premier points, a cat must earn a best-cat-in-show win.

Nonchampionship Competition

CCA also offers classes for kittens, household pets, and breeds not yet accepted for championship competition. (The latter compete in experimental classes.) The cats in those categories do not compete for titles, but kittens can compete for regional and national year-end awards, while household pets can compete for regional year-end awards.

Regional and National Awards

Annual awards are calculated for the top 15 cats, the top ten kittens, and the top ten alters. To be eligible for a CCA national award, a cat, kitten or alter must score at least 100 points by the end of the show season. Points are awarded to cats that finish among the top ten cats in show or are selected best or second best of breed. Regional awards are also presented to the top 15 household pets in the Quebec and Ontario regions.

Differently Abled Cats

Declawed cats cannot be shown in championship or alter classes in CCA. Neither can blind cats or cats that have lost all or part of an ear, limb, or tail because of accident or injury be shown in either of these categories. Deaf cats may be shown in championship and alter classes.

The Cat Fanciers' Association

Championship Competition

The Cat Fanciers' Association (CFA) offers championship competi-

tion for unaltered, pedigreed cats that are registered with CFA and are at least eight months old on the opening day of the show. The following two titles can be earned in championship competition in CFA: champion, grand champion. The requirements for those titles are:

Champion: Six winner's ribbons from at least four different judges. Cats that have not earned their championships compete for winner's ribbons in the open class against other members of their breed and sex. To earn a winner's ribbon a cat must finish first in his class. In Hawaii, four winner's ribbons won under at least three different judges are required for championship.

Grand champion: 200 grand champion points earned under three different judges. Cats competing for the grand champion title are entered in the champion class. A cat earns grand champion points by winning the best champion of breed or division award in competition. Cats

At the year end award ceremonies, everyone, including the cats, comes dressed in their best.

winning that award earn one grand champion point for every other champion they defeated that was also competing for best champion in that breed or division. Cats can also earn grand champion points by being selected one of the ten best cats in show, even if they were not the best champion in their breeds or divisions. A champion placing among the top ten cats in show receives one grand championship point for each champion it defeated in competition at that show. If another champion also makes the top ten finalists, that cat receives 90 percent of the points awarded to the highest placing champion. All other champions placing in the top ten— from the third-best champion to the tenth-best champion in the extremely rare event that all top ten cats are champions—would receive grand championship points according to a sliding scale that proceeds in decreasing 10 percent increments. Thus, the third-best champion receives 80 percent of the best champion's point total; the fourth-best 70 percent, and so on, all the way down to the tenth-best champion, who would receive 10 percent of the best champion's point total.

In addition to earning 200 grand points, a cat must win at least one best champion or second best champion in show award. In lieu of that, however, a cat may place once among the top ten best cats in show in either an allbreed or a specialty ring. (In Japan, only 100 grand champion points are required to win the grand champion title. In Hawaii, 75 points are required.)

Premiership (Alter) Competition

CFA offers premiership competition for altered, pedigreed cats that are registered with CFA and are at least eight months old on the opening day of the show. The following two titles can be earned in premiership competition in CFA: premier, grand premier. The requirements for those titles are:

Premier: six winner's ribbons from at least four different judges. Cats that have not earned their premierships compete in the open class against other members of their sex and breed. A cat earns a winner's ribbon by winning her class. In Hawaii, four winner's ribbons won under at least three different judges are required.

Grand premier: 75 grand premier points earned under three different judges. Cats competing for the grand premier title are entered in the premier class, where they earn grand premier points by winning the best premier of breed or division award in competition. Cats winning that award earn one grand premier point for every other premier they defeated that was also competing for best premier of breed or division. Cats can also earn grand premier points by being selected one of the ten best cats in show, even if they were not the best premier in their breeds or divisions. A premier placing among the top ten cats in show receives one grand premiership point for each premier it defeated in competition at that show. If another premier also makes the top ten finalists, that cat receives 90 percent of the points awarded to the highest placing premier. All other premiers placing in the top ten—from the third-best premier to the tenth-best premier in the extremely rare event that all top ten cats are premiers—would receive grand premiership points according to a sliding scale that proceeds in decreasing 10 percent increments. Thus, the third-best premier receives 80 percent of the best premier's point total; the fourth-best 70 percent, and so on, all the way down to the tenth-best premier, who would receive 10 percent of the best premier's point total.

In addition to earning 200 grand premier points, a cat must win at least one best premier or second best premier in show award. In lieu of that, however, a cat may place once among the top ten best cats in show in either an allbreed or a specialty ring.

Only 25 grand premier points are required to win the grand premier title in Hawaii. Thirty-five points are required to win that title in Japan.

Nonchampionship Competition

CFA also offers competition for kittens, household pets, and breeds that have not yet been accepted for championship competition. Kittens do not compete for titles, but they can compete for regional and

The judge tempts the cat with a toy to check its alertness and movement.

national year-end awards. Household pets do not compete for either titles or year-end awards.

Regional and National Awards

Annual awards, both regional and national, are awarded to the 25 highest scoring cats, the 20 highest scoring kittens, and 20 highest scoring premiers during the show season. Cats, kittens, and premiers earn points toward those awards by defeating others of their ilk in competition during the show season. The best cat, kitten, or premier in show receives one point for each competing entry defeated. The second-best cat, kitten, or premier receives 95 percent of the points awarded to the best contestant in that category. Third- through tenth-best cats, kittens, or premiers

ANIMAL SHELTER
NAME: Tasha
BREED: Persian
AGE: 6 months old
REASON FOR SURRENDER:
Owner could not
take care of so
many kittens
HEALTH RECORD:
Perfect health

NOTES: Very sweet
cat—loves people

Behind every cat in a shelter is a human who did not live up to the responsibilities of cat ownership. This sweet cat deserves a loving home and with a little TLC might become a winner in the household pet category.

receive points in decreasing, 5 percent increments from 90 percent of the best cat's total points (third-best cat) to 55 percent (tenth-best cat). The best cat of each breed or division receives one point for each competing cat defeated within that breed or division. Second-best of breed or division receives 95 percent of the points awarded to the best of breed or division.

Differently Abled Cats

Although declawed cats cannot be exhibited in any class in CFA, blind and deaf cats are eligible to compete. Cats or kittens missing eyes, ears, legs, or tails—except for breeds such as the Manx whose standards call for a missing or abbreviated part—are not eligible for CFA classes.

Cat Fanciers' Federation

In the Cat Fanciers' Federation (CFF), championship competition is open to unaltered, pedigreed cats that are at least eight months old on the opening day of the show. A cat does not have to be registered with CFF in order to be shown in a championship class as long as that cat has been registered with ACA, ACFA, CCA, CFA, the Governing Council of the Cat Fancy in England, or the Federation Internationale Féline (FIFe) in Europe. There is no limit to the number of times an unregistered cat can be shown in CFF, but a cat cannot begin to earn any winner's ribbons or points toward various titles until it is registered.

The following three titles can be earned in championship competition in CFF: champion, grand champion, master grand champion. The requirements for those titles are:

Championship Competition

Champion: four winner's ribbons under at least three different judges. In Hawaii a cat must win two winner's ribbons under two different judges. Cats that have not yet earned their championships compete for winner's ribbons against other members of their breed and sex in the open class. A cat earns a winner's ribbon by winning her class.

Grand champion: 150 grand champion points earned under at least three different judges. Cats hoping to earn a grand championship compete in the champion class. A cat earns grand champion points by winning the best- through fifth-best-champion-in-show award.

In a specialty show the best champion receives one point for each competing champion it defeated in the show. The second-best champion in show receives one point fewer than the best champion. The third-best champion receives 75 percent of the points received by the second-best champion. The fourth-best champion wins 50 percent of the points received by the second-best champion, and the fifth-best champion receives 25 percent of the points received by the second-best champion. (In allbreed shows, these awards are given to the best through fifth-best longhair champions and the best through fifth-best shorthair champions.)

In addition to earning 150 grand champion points, a cat must have been judged among the top five cats at least once in one allbreed or specialty show in order to become a grand champion.

Master grand champion: 100 master grand champion points awarded by at least six different judges and one best-cat-in-show win in either an allbreed or a specialty ring. The best cat award must be earned after a cat has become a grand champion. Any best-cat wins earned as a champion or an open do not count toward the master grand champion title. Cats competing for

their master grand championships are entered in the grand champion class.

Alter Competition

In CFF, alter competition is open to altered, pedigreed cats that are at least eight months old on the opening day of the show. A cat does not have to be registered with CFF in order to be shown in an alter class as long as that cat has been registered with ACA, ACFA, CCA, CFA, the Governing Council of the Cat Fancy in England, or the Federation Internationale Féline (FIFe) in Europe. There is no limit to the number of times an unregistered cat can be shown in CFF, but a cat cannot begin to earn any winner's ribbons or points toward various titles until it is registered.

The following three titles can be earned in alter competition in CFF: champion, grand champion, master grand champion. The requirements for those titles are:

Champion: Four winner's ribbons under at least three different judges. In Hawaii a cat must win two winner's ribbons under two different judges. Cats that have not yet earned their championships compete for winner's ribbons against other members of their breed and sex in the open class. A cat earns a winner's ribbon by winning his class.

Grand champion: 80 grand champion points earned under at least three different judges. Cats hoping to earn a grand championship compete in the champion

class. A cat earns grand champion points by winning the best- through fifth-best-champion-in-show award.

In a specialty show the best champion receives one point for each competing champion it defeated in the show. The second-best champion in show receives one point fewer than the best champion. The third-best champion receives 75 percent of the points received by the second-best champion. The fourth-best champion wins 50 percent of the points received by the second-best champion, and the fifth-best champion receives 25 percent of the points received by the second-best champion. (In allbreed shows, these awards are given to the best through fifth-best longhair champions and the best through fifth-best shorthair champions.)

In addition to earning 80 grand champion points, a cat must have been judged among the top five cats in one allbreed or specialty show at least once in order to become a grand champion.

Master grand champion: 75 master grand champion points awarded by at least six different judges and one best-cat-in-show win in either an allbreed or a specialty ring. The best cat award must be earned after a cat has become a grand champion. Any best-cat wins earned as a champion or an open do not count toward the master grand champion title. Cats competing for their master grand championships are entered in the grand champion class.

Nonchampionship Competition

CFF also offers classes for kittens, household pets, and breeds that have not yet been accepted for championship competition. Kittens do not compete for titles, but they can earn regional and national year-end awards. Household pets can earn titles and compete for year-end regional and national awards. Cats that have not yet been accepted for championship competition are shown in the provisional class. They do not compete for titles, but they can win year-end awards.

Regional and National Awards

A graduated point scale based on how high a cat places in finals is used to determine parade of perfection winners in CFF. Parade of perfection winners are the 20 highest scoring cats, kittens, and alters that competed in the association during the previous feline year.

Differently Abled Cats

Declawed cats cannot be shown in championship or alter classes in CFF. Show rules are silent regarding the exhibition of deaf and blind cats. Cats that are deformed or disfigured as a result of a hereditary, congenital, or acquired condition cannot be exhibited.

The International Cat Association

Championship Competition

The International Cat Association (TICA) offers championship competition to unaltered, pedigreed cats that are at least eight months old on the opening day of the show. A cat does not have to be registered with TICA in order to be shown in a championship class, but any points or awards the cat wins at that show are lost if the cat is not registered with TICA by the next time it competes in a TICA show.

The following six titles can be earned in championship competition in TICA: champion, grand champion, double grand champion, triple grand champion, quadruple grand champion, and supreme grand champion. The requirements for those titles are:

Champion: 300 points under no fewer than four different judges (in Alaska, Hawaii, and Japan, only 150 points are required under no fewer

than two different judges), and one placement among the top ten cats in show in either an allbreed or a specialty ring. Cats that have not earned their championships yet compete in the novice class.

Grand champion: 1,000 points under at least four different judges. Cats that have earned their championships are entered in the champion class, where they compete for grand champion points. In addition to earning 1,000 grand points, a cat must be selected among the top ten cats in show at least three times in allbreed competition. Three additional final wins are required, and these may be top-ten allbreed wins or top-five specialty wins. In Alaska, Hawaii, and Japan only 500 points are required under two different judges, and the cat must earn at least one top-ten allbreed win or top-five final specialty win in addition to two other finishes among the top ten cats in either an allbreed or a specialty show.

Double grand champion: 1,000 additional points and selection at least once among the top ten cats in an allbreed ring or the top five cats in a specialty ring. In Alaska, Hawaii, and Japan only 500 points are required.

Triple grand champion: same as for double grand champion.

Quadruple grand champion: same as for double grand champion.

Supreme grand champion: After completing the requirements for a quadruple grand championship, a cat must earn 2,000 additional points and an additional (or first) best-cat-in-show award. In Alaska, Hawaii, and Japan only 1,000 points are required.

Alter Competition

The International Cat Association (TICA) offers alter competition to altered, pedigreed cats that are at least eight months old on the first day of the show. A cat does not have to be registered with TICA in order to be shown in an alter class, but any points or awards the cat wins at that show are lost if the cat is not registered with TICA by the next time it competes in a TICA show.

The following six titles can be earned in alter competition in TICA: champion, grand champion, double

grand champion, triple grand champion, quadruple grand champion, and supreme grand champion. The requirements for those titles are:

Champion: 300 points under no fewer than four different judges, (in Alaska, Hawaii, and Japan, only 150 points are required under no fewer than two different judges), and one placement among the top ten cats in either an allbreed or a specialty show. Cats that have not earned their championships yet compete in the novice class.

Grand champion: 1,000 points under at least four different judges. Cats that have earned their championships are entered in the champion class, where they compete for grand champion points. In addition to earning 1,000 grand points, a cat must be selected among the top ten cats in show at least three times in allbreed competition. Three additional final wins are required, and these may be top-ten allbreed wins or top-five specialty wins. In Alaska, Hawaii, and Japan only 500 points are required under two different judges, and the cat must earn at least one top-ten allbreed win or top-five final specialty win in addition to two other finishes among the top ten cats in either an allbreed or a specialty show.

Double grand champion: 1,000 additional points and selection at least once among the top ten cats in an allbreed ring or the top five cats in a specialty ring. In Alaska, Hawaii, and Japan only 500 points are required.

These rosettes are displayed on racks for all to see.

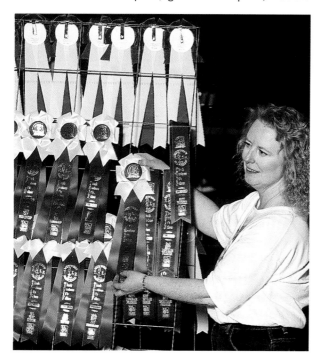

Triple grand champion: same as for double grand champion.

Quadruple grand champion: same as for double grand champion.

Supreme grand champion: after completing the requirements for a quadruple grand championship, a cat must earn 2,000 additional points and an additional (or first) best-cat-in-show award. In Alaska, Hawaii, and Japan only 1,000 points are required.

Nonchampionship Competition

TICA also offers classes for kittens, household pets, and breeds that have not yet been accepted for championship competition. Kittens do not compete for titles, but they can earn regional and national awards. Household pets compete for titles and regional and national awards.

Regional and National Awards

In calculating regional and national awards TICA's executive office sums the points earned by each registered cat, alter, kitten, and household pet during the show year. Those points are earned by placing among the top ten cats in show. The cats with the greatest number of points are the winners of the various awards offered. No matter how many times a cat or alter has been shown during the show year, TICA counts only the points from that cat's 50 highest scoring performances. Kitten and household pet awards are based on a contestant's 30 highest scoring performances during the show season.

Differently Abled Cats

Deaf or blind cats cannot be shown in championship or alter competition in TICA. Declawed cats or cats that have lost all or part of an ear, limb, or tail because of accident or injury can be shown in these categories.

Traditional Cat Association

Championship Competition

In the Traditional Cat Association (TCA) championship competition is open to unaltered, pedigreed cats that are at least eight months old on the first day of the show. A cat does not have to be registered with TCA in order to be shown in a championship class as long as that cat has been registered with one of the following cat associations: ACA, ACFA, CCA, CFA, CFF, and TICA.

The following titles can be earned in championship competition in TCA: champion, grand champion. The requirements for those titles are:

Champion: four winner's ribbons under three different judges. In Hawaii two winner's ribbons under two different judges are required. Cats that have not yet earned their championships compete in the open class against other members of their breed and sex. A cat earns a winner's ribbon by placing first in her class.

Grand champion: 150 grand champion points. In Hawaii 50 points are required. In Japan 75 points are required for grand championship. The points must be won under three different judges. In addition a cat must be selected best or second-best champion in at least one show, or else a cat must be selected among the ten best cats in a specialty or allbreed show.

Cats seeking to earn a grand championship are entered in the champion class. A cat earns grand champion points by being selected best or second-best champion in show. In a specialty show the best champion receives one point for every other champion defeated in competition. The second-best champion receives 90 percent of the points awarded to the best champion. Other champions, even if they are not selected best or second-best champion in show, can earn points toward their grand championships by being selected among the top ten cats in show. The third-best champion receives 80 percent of the points awarded to the best champion. Fourth best receives 70 percent of the best champion's points, and so on, all the way down to the tenth-best champion, who receives 10 percent of the points won by the best champion, in the rare event that all cats in finals were champions.

In allbreed shows the best longhair champion receives one point for every other longhair champion defeated in the show, and the second-best longhair champion receives 90 percent of the points won by the best longhair champion. What's more, the best shorthair champion receives one point for every other shorthair champion defeated in the show, and the second-best shorthair champion receives 90 percent of the points won by the best shorthair champion.

Premier Competition

In the Traditional Cat Association (TCA) premier competition is open to altered, pedigreed cats that are at least eight months old on the opening day of the show. A cat does not have to be registered with TCA in order to be shown in a premier class as long as that cat has been registered with one of the following cat associations: ACA, ACFA, CCA, CFA, CFF, and TICA.

The following titles can be earned in premiership competition in TCA: premier, grand premier. The requirements for those titles are:

Premier: four winner's ribbons under three different judges. In Hawaii two winner's ribbons under two different judges are required. Cats that have not yet earned their premierships compete against other members of their breed and sex in the open class, where they earn winner's ribbons by placing first in the class.

Grand premier: 75 grand premier points under three different judges. In Hawaii 25 points are required. In Japan 35 points are required for grand premiership. In addition a cat must be selected best or second-best champion in at least one show, or else a cat must be selected among the ten best cats in a specialty or allbreed show.

Cats compete for points toward their grand premierships in the premier class. A cat earns grand premier points by being selected best or second-best premier in show. In shorthair specialty shows the best premier receives one point for every other premier defeated in competition. The second-best premier receives 90 percent of the points awarded to the best premier. Other premiers, even if they are not selected best or second-best premier in show, can earn points toward their grand premierships by being selected among the top ten cats in show. The third-best premier receives 80 percent of the points awarded to the best premier. Fourth best receives 70 percent of the best premier's points, and so on, all the way down to the tenth-best premier, who receives 10 percent of the points won by the best premier, in the rare event that all cats in finals were premier.

In allbreed shows the best longhair premier receives one point for every other longhair premier defeated in the show, and the second-best longhair premier receives 90 percent of the points won by the best longhair premier. What's more, the best shorthair premier receives one point for every other shorthair premier defeated in the show, and the second-best shorthair premier receives 90 percent of the points won by the best shorthair premier.

Nonchampionship Competition

TCA also offers classes for kittens, household pets, and breeds not yet accepted for championship competition. Kittens do not compete for titles, but they can earn regional and national year-end awards. Household pets compete for titles and regional and national year-end awards.

Regional and National Awards

Cats, kittens, premiers, and household pets are eligible for regional and national awards in TCA. Every time a cat makes a final in TCA she wins points toward a national or regional award. Those points are awarded based on how high a cat places in finals and the number of other cats it defeats in the show. The points earned by each cat that makes finals at a TCA show are converted to an average ring

This exhibitor is delighted with her cat's winning ribbon, but her cat companion looks bushed from a long day of showing.

score for that show. In calculating a cat's total points for the season, TCA allows only the 100 highest ring averages for each cat or the 40 highest ring averages for each kitten.

United Feline Organization

In the United Feline Organization (UFO) championship competition is open to unaltered, pedigreed cats that are at least eight months old on the first day of the show. A cat may be exhibited in one UFO show without being registered with the association. After that, cats must be registered in order to compete.

Championship Competition

The following four titles can be earned in championship competition in UFO: champion, silver grand champion, golden grand champion, and platinum grand champion. The requirements for those titles are:

Champion: Nonchampion cats that are competing to earn points toward their championships are entered in the open class. To achieve the title of champion in UFO a cat must accumulate 150 points under at least four different judges.

Silver Grand Champion

Once a cat has completed the requirements for championship, it is eligible to compete in the champion class, where it can earn points toward its silver grand championship. To become a silver grand champion a cat must earn 2,000 points. In addition the cat must be selected among the top ten cats in show 12 times under at least six different judges. (In at least three of those finals the cat must place fifth-best cat or higher in either a specialty or an allbreed show.)

Golden Grand Champion

Once a cat completes the requirements for the silver grand championship, it is eligible to earn points and awards toward its golden grand championship. To earn the title of golden grand champion, a cat must accumulate 4,000 points. In addition the cat must be in finals at least 24 times under at least ten different judges. In at least three of those finals the cat must be third best cat or higher in a specialty or an allbreed ring.

Platinum Grand Champion

Once a cat has completed the requirements for the golden grand championship, it is eligible to compete for points and awards toward its platinum grand championship. To become a platinum grand champion, a cat must accumulate 6,000 points. In addition, the cat must be in finals at least 30 times under at least 12 different judges. Of these finals, the cat must earn two Best in Shows in allbreed rings and four Best Specialty in specialty rings. Or, in addition to the two Best in Show titles, the other four titles can be a combination of two Best in Show and two Best Specialty.

Alter Competition

In UFO alter competition is open to altered, pedigreed cats that are at least eight months old on the first day of the show. A cat may be exhibited in one UFO show without being registered with the association. After that, cats must be registered in order to compete.

The following four titles can be earned in championship competition in UFO: imperial, silver imperial, golden imperial, and platinum imperial. The requirements for those titles are:

Imperial: Cats that have not yet earned their imperialships compete in the open class against other members of their breed and sex for points toward that title. To achieve the title of imperial in UFO a cat must accumulate 150 points under at least four different judges.

Silver Imperial: Once a cat has completed the requirements for imperialship, it is eligible to earn points toward its silver imperialship. To become a silver imperial a cat must earn 2,000 points. In addition the cat must be selected among the top ten cats in show 12 times under at least six different judges. (In at least three of those finals the cat must place fifth-best cat or higher in either a specialty or an allbreed show.)

Golden Imperial: Once a cat completes the requirements for the silver imperial title, it is eligible to compete for points and awards toward its golden imperialship. To earn the title of golden imperial, a cat must accumulate 4,000 points. In addition the cat must be in finals at least 24 times under at least ten different judges. (In at least three of those finals the cat must be third-best cat or higher in a specialty or an allbreed ring.)

Platinum Imperial: Once a cat has completed the requirements for the golden imperial title, it is eligible to compete for points and awards toward its platinum imperialship. To become a platinum imperial a cat must accumulate 6,000 points. In addition the cat must be in finals at least 30 times under at least 12 different judges. The cat must be Best Allbreed in two of these finals and Best Specialty in four finals, or a combination of two Best in Show in an Allbreed ring and two Best Specialty.

Nonchampionship Competition

UFO also offers classes for kittens, household pets, and breeds not yet accepted for championship competition.

Differently Abled Cats

Declawed cats and deaf cats can be shown in all classes in UFO shows. Blind cats and cats that have lost all or part of an ear, limb, or tail because of accident or injury cannot be shown in UFO.

Regional and National Wins

Regional and national year-end awards are given to the highest scoring cats, kittens, alters, and household pets. The awards are

Have I earned enough points for the Top-20?

based on the points a cat earns every time it makes a final at a UFO show. Only their highest scoring 24 rings are included in the calculations for national year-end awards for kittens, cats, alters, and household pets. The national and regional awards presented in the United States include the top-20 cats, kittens, alters, and household pets and the top ten in new-breed competition. In addition awards are presented to the top-ten cats, kittens, alters, and household pets in Japan.

Chapter 8
Provisions for a Show

Don't be afraid to take a big step if one is indicated; you can't cross a chasm in two small jumps.

—David Lloyd George

You have managed, with the aid of the muscle provided by a hefty check, to pry a show cat loose from a breeder. You have staggered your way through the alphabet soup of organizations that sanction cat shows, and you have chosen one in which you think your cat will be competitive. You have registered a cattery name and a name for your cat. (Hopefully it is not a name that will make you cringe in later years.) You have located and entered a cat show; you think you know how wins are scored and titles are earned in the organization sanctioning that show; and you feel confident that your cat will not look like something the cat dragged in after you finish grooming it. Now it is time to make a checklist of things you will need to take to that show.

Passports

The best laid plans of many exhibitors, novice and veteran alike,

are ruined by the discovery, usually made just past the halfway point to the show hall, that the cat's confirmation letter is sitting at home in the top drawer of the desk in the den. Pack the confirmation letter the night before the show. Pack your cat's rabies certificate and any other health certificates the show requires at the same time.

Food and Water

Some shows provide cat food for exhibitors' cats, but many cats develop an attitude about eating strange food in a strange place. You

Shows held near holidays inspire some exhibitors to get into the "spirit" of things.

can control one of those variables if you pack your cat's favorite food.

Because virtually all show halls have indoor plumbing these days, water is also available on site. Chances are good that your cat will find the water suitable and that the water will not upset your cat's stomach. If you want to raise those odds, however, bring a supply of your cat's drinking water from home.

Bowls and Dishes

Unless your cat is used to eating from a dish or bowl the size of the Grand Canyon at home, bring his bowl to the show. If you decide to buy a special, smaller dish or bowl for the show, keep cage size in mind (see page 92) when making your

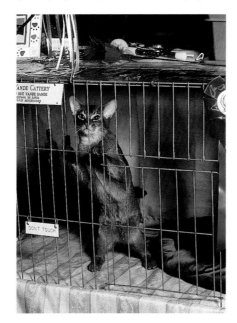

Your cat will be more comfortable if you decorate the cage with familiar toys and bedding.

purchase. Remember that reusable plastic ware can retain odors even if washed carefully, and disposable plastic is a burden on the environment. Glass, ceramic, or metal are the best choices. All plates and bowls should be solid and heavy enough not to tip over easily. Almost all exhibitors prefer water cups that attach to the side of the cat's cage. Available at cat shows or from animal supply houses, these cups all but eliminate the possibility that your cat will spill its water, and they significantly reduce the chances that your cat will drag its tail through its water.

Miscellaneous Utensils

If you have packed canned food for your cat, you will need a fork or spoon, you may need a can opener, and a rubber lid for the can if you do not serve the entire can at once. A small place mat might also be helpful if your cat likes to remove her food from the bowl or dish to inspect the food carefully before eating it.

Litter Pan and Litter

Most shows provide litter pans and litter. In the event that your show is one of the rare ones that does not—or if you are afraid your cat will not want to sully its feet on strange litter—bring a supply of acceptable litter from home and a small litter pan. Three or four disposable cardboard litter pans, which should be available at a pet supply store, will be sufficient. If the cage at the show is small, cut a disposable cardboard pan in half vertically and fold it back together. (Some exhibitors prefer small plastic pans or plastic food-storage containers.)

Waste-Removal Tools

A litter scoop, the sturdier the better, is a must-have item. Plastic bags for packaging soiled litter before disposing of it are a must also. Litter pan liners, though they are not always practical for extended use at home because cats frequently poke holes in them, are convenient for bundling up the contents of the pan and discarding them during motel stays.

Grooming Aids

Most show grooming should be done at home. If a cat has been bathed and groomed properly before a show, his owner won't need to haul the full-battlefield grooming regalia to the show hall. Indeed, exhibitors of most shorthaired cats shouldn't need much more than a comb or two, a brush, and a chamois. Exhibitors of longhairs will need combs and

Bring along grooming supplies for a last-minute touch up while you wait for your number to be called.

brushes, cotton swabs, cotton balls, grooming powder, fresh water (for cleaning faces), and a small container in which to put it.

All exhibitors will need a place to groom their cats. A small, TV-dinner-sized table is useful in this regard for novice exhibitors. A bath towel makes a good cover for the table. People who decide to make a habit out of showing may prefer a more sturdy arrangement, for example, a metal grooming table that clips to the trestle supporting the benching cage in the show hall.

Because clip-on metal tables may not be useable at all shows, some exhibitors prefer tables that consist of two carpeted platforms, one of which has castors affixed to its bottom. The castored platform fits under a cat carrier. The other carpeted platform goes on top of the carrier. The whole arrangement is secured with bungee cords. Exhibitors usually stack one cat carrier on top of the other to raise the grooming table to a more comfortable height. Exhibitors showing only one cat can use the empty carrier for storing supplies and—if the carrier can be locked—valuables too large to carry around at a show.

A grooming table made of stacked cages topped with a sturdy carpet-covered board is convenient and easy to transport. Bungee cords hold the cages in place.

Cleaning Materials

Nonammonia-based disinfectant and paper towels are needed for wiping down the benching cage and any suspicious surfaces in the hotel room. (Some exhibitors use disinfectant towelettes for these purposes.)

Emergency Bathing Materials

Emergencies will happen at cat shows. A longhaired cat will upset her water dish and lie in the resulting puddle. A cat will crawl under the bed at the hotel and come out covered with dust bunnies. Therefore, many exhibitors travel with a hair drier, a supply of towels, a spray attachment, and the fervent hope that it will fit the hotel faucet.

Cage Furnishings

Exhibitors are expected to bring curtains for the sides and back of the benching cage and a rug or a towel for the cage floor. Most single show cages are small: 22 inches (56 cm) long, wide, and tall. For an extra $10 to $20, exhibitors can order a double cage when they send in their entry blanks. A double cage provides more room in which a cat can stretch its legs, and the extra chair that comes with a double cage provides a convenient footrest for an exhibitor. Most double cages are 22 inches (56 cm) deep and tall and 44 inches (112 cm) wide.

Cage decorations vary with an exhibitor's taste, budget, sewing ability, and sense of style. Some exhibitors equip their cages with lavish, hand-sewn curtains and four-poster beds. Other exhibitors fancy a military-barracks look with bath towels held in place by metal clamps. (Pipe cleaners are handy for

Some exhibitors bring their own enclosures to discourage lookers from touching the cats and to help prevent the spread of disease.

securing any loose corners of the cage.)

A few exhibitors bring their own cages, which often resemble a cross between a habitrail for cats and a miniature intensive-care unit. Personal aesthetics notwithstanding, minimum show requirements decree that cage curtains be fastened securely inside the cage and that they cover both the sides and the back of the cage. Many exhibitors also cover the tops of their cages, creating a more cozy environment for their cats.

Cat Carrier

Cats should be transported to shows in sturdy, molded plastic carriers. These are available at pet supply stores, pet shops, some airline cargo offices, and cat shows. The cat's journey will be more

To save money, some exhibitors bring their own food and drinks in coolers; make sure this is allowed beforehand. If not, food and drinks are available at stands in the show hall.

Basic Show Supplies

adhesive tape
antistatic clothes-drier
  sheets
bath towels
biodegradable paper plates
bottle opener
bottled water from home
brushes and grooming
  powder if applicable
cage and carrier locks
cage curtains
cage rug
can opener
cardboard litter pans
cat food
cat shampoo
cat toys
cattery business cards
cellophane tape

coat conditioners
cooler (if permitted)
cotton balls
cotton swabs
entry confirmation
eye drops
facial tissues
first-aid kit
flea comb
litter scoop
magazine, book, or
  small TV
masking tape
nail clippers
paper towels
pipe cleaners
regular combs
safety pins
saline solution

scissors
small cat bed
small metal clamps
small plastic baggies
small, TV-dinner-sized table
small whisk broom and
  dustpan
snacks and hors d'oeuvres
spoon
spray disinfectant
sweater and sweatpants
  (in case the show hall is
  cold)
washcloths
water bowl
wristwatch
writing pen

comfortable, especially if the ride is long or the cat is young, if the owner tapes a small litter pan to the floor inside the carrier. Disposable cardboard litter pans, cut in half (with the cut parallel to the shorter sides) and folded back together, fit easily into a carrier. The rest of the carrier floor should be covered with a towel or disposable diaper.

Many exhibitors cover the outside of their carriers with fitted, quilted bonnets in cold weather. These bonnets, which resemble toaster covers, are available at shows or from companies that advertise in cat magazines. Exhibitors also can sew their own.

Show Supply Checklist

Like fashions in cage curtains, the number of incidental items packed for a show is determined by personal comfort. Some exhibitors trundle into a show hall with enough provisions for a two-month stay in a biosphere. Others pack more conservatively. The list above, as they say at commencement exercises, is not an end, it's a beginning. You will need some of the items on this list all the time and all of the items some of the time. You will not need all of the items all of the time. Modify the list as you wish.

Chapter 9
The Art of Cat Grooming

One cannot woo a cat after the fashion of the conqueror. Courtesy, tact, patience are needed at every step . . .
—*Agnes Repplier*

Cats are naturally clean animals. They devote a good portion of their day to grooming themselves. They have even been equipped with a tongue covered with hooked, backward-pointing scales called papillae, which make the tongue a carry-everywhere tool for combing the fur and skin. Most cats need some help from their human companions to keep looking sharp, however, and grooming is particularly important for the show cat, who must look her absolute best before heading to the show hall.

Establish a grooming routine early in the cat's life. Grooming can be a pleasant experience for you and your cat if you train her to tolerate grooming when she is young. Cats are creatures of habit—establish a regular grooming schedule so your cat knows what to expect. Preferably, you should start a grooming

program when your cat is three months old. Your cat will come to expect and even enjoy her grooming sessions. She will learn to tolerate a regular grooming schedule much better than if you bathe and groom the cat only when you're preparing for a show. A regular grooming program is also good for a cat's health. Grooming removes dead hair that can form hair balls in a cat's stomach (as well as on your couch), gets

Perfect grooming can be the difference between winning and losing. This lovely white Persian is beautifully groomed.

rid of dead skin and dander, stimulates the skin, tones muscles, and encourages blood circulation. It is also a good opportunity to examine your cat for developing health problems and to attend to them in their early stages. Since the physical condition of the show cat is as important as her conformation, coat, and color, it's important to keep on top of any developing health problems. Cats must be free of fleas, ticks, lice, mites, fungus, and other infectious conditions to be exhibited.

A Grooming Schedule

A cat's grooming schedule is determined by its breed and the proximity of its next show. Preparations for a show must begin well in

A good quality stainless steel comb is a grooming must. This Somali's fur is being back-combed.

advance of the first call to the ring if a cat is to make a good impression on the judges. There are no two ways about it, a show cat must look her absolute best. A show cat in top condition must be physically fit and healthy, temperamentally amenable to handling, and flawlessly groomed. Therefore, most exhibitors spend considerable time grooming, bathing, and preening their cats before a show. After a thorough combing, they bathe their cats, using shampoos and conditioners that make the coat look its best. After combing, washing, and blow drying the coat— and combing again—they backcomb to add body. They meticulously clean the eyes, ears, and face with cotton balls and swabs. For the show cat and her owner, bathing and grooming become a way of life.

For the purposes of a discussion of grooming, purebred cats can be assigned into one of three general categories: longhairs, semilonghairs, and shorthairs. Longhairs in general require a good deal more grooming than shorthaired breeds do. Persians and Himalayans, for example, require daily grooming if their long luxurious coats are to be kept free of mats and snarls. Semilonghairs that lack the thick double coat of the Persian (e.g., cats such as the Balinese, Oriental Longhair, and Turkish Angora), should be groomed every other day. Shorthaired cats such as Siamese and Burmese can get by on one or two grooming sessions per week. All breeds should be bathed before each show. It's wise to ask your breeder for grooming tips regarding your particular breed. Some, such as the Sphynx, American Wirehair, and Rex breeds have special grooming requirements, and your breeder can advise you about them.

Many cats, particularly longhaired cats such as the Maine Coon and the Norwegian Forest Cat, go through two distinct periods in which they shed heavily—in the spring when they shed their longer, heavier winter coats, and again in the fall before growing their winter coats again. For these breeds it's important to groom out the dead hairs daily while the cats are shedding.

Grooming Tools

The most important grooming tool is a good-quality stainless steel comb with teeth about 1¼ inches long. The teeth on one half of the comb are very close together. The teeth on the other half are spaced farther apart. The Greyhound comb, available at pet and grooming supply stores, is one that some professional groomers and breeders favor. This comb effectively removes dead and loose hairs, but doesn't damage a cat's fur. Combs coated with Teflon are also available. These prevent static electricity from building up during grooming. A grooming rake is also a good investment. This comb looks much like a miniature rake (thus the name) and is easy to handle. Whatever comb you buy, be

sure the teeth are rounded rather than pointed so you don't hurt your cat during the grooming session. Don't buy wire slicker type brushes because they can damage your cat's coat. They also slide over rather than loosen developing mats. It's wise to purchase a flea comb as well. These combs come in metal or plastic, but the metal variety is the better choice. The teeth on a flea comb are tightly packed (usually 22 to 36 teeth per inch) to catch the fleas and flea dirt between the tines and to draw them out of the fur.

Other necessary items are mat breakers for longhaired breeds (some exhibitors use a sewing seam ripper for this job) and blunt-tip scissors for cutting stubborn mats, a soft bristle cat brush, a rubber curry brush, cotton balls, cotton swabs, a face cloth, cat nail clippers, a child-size toothbrush, and a trash can or other receptacle.

Optional supplies include hairball preventive, grooming powder (you

Bathing your cat will be easier if you gather the required materials beforehand.

can also use baby powder), coat conditioner, a chamois cloth, and tear-stain remover. A grooming table is also an option if you want to keep your tables and counters free of cat hair, but it isn't a necessity if you do not have space available or if you have an old, steady table that you can use for grooming. Don't use a table or counter where the cat is normally not allowed, however. Not only will this confuse your cat, but putting your cat on a surface where she knows she's not supposed to be will make her uncomfortable and make the grooming session more stressful for her. This may also give her the idea that it's okay to snooze on that table or surface after all.

When cleaning your cat's ears, be careful not to push the swab into the ear canal.

Always buy good quality grooming supplies. They will last for your cat's lifetime and are well worth the money. Consult your breeder, groomer, or veterinarian for recommendations, or ask for advice at a well-stocked pet supply store or grooming aids distributor. Most necessary products can be found in pet supply stores, but some specialty items may only be available from a grooming supply store or a pet supply catalog.

Other Grooming Products

You can buy any number of products to keep your cat from having a bad hair day. The same types of products sold for styling human hair are available for your cat's tresses, including dyes and hot-oil treatments. Believe it or not, there's even a styling mousse made for cats to add body to the fur, and it works essentially the same as it would on a person with long, fine hair. How many and which products you use depend upon the length of your cat's hair, the condition of her coat and skin, your grooming enthusiasm, and your pocketbook.

Shampoos. Protein shampoos combat dryness, condition the coat, and build body. Tearless shampoos don't irritate the cat's eyes the way ordinary shampoos can. They are recommended for cats. Medicated shampoos relieve minor skin conditions such as dryness and flaking. If your cat has oily fur, degreasers help rid the coat of excessive oil, grease, and dirt. Herbal shampoos are available, as well as those containing oatmeal to soothe itchy skin, reduce static cling, and restore natural moisture. Coat brightening shampoos enhance the coat's color and add brilliance and sparkle to the coat. Hypoallergenic shampoos are available for cats with sensitive skin. Finally, dry shampoos absorb the dirt and oil without water. These are good if your cat has a violent aversion to bathing.

Tick and flea shampoos, of course, kill parasites. Be sure parasites are actually present before you use these products, and be sure the label says "safe for cats." If the label does not, don't use the product on your cat. Insecticide levels safe for dogs can be harmful or even fatal to cats.

Rinses. Rinses untangle the coat, leaving it smooth. They also add body and help to cut down on static electricity in your cat's coat. Detanglers loosen mats and make combing easier.

Coat conditioners. These products contain ingredients to condition and revitalize dry coats, add body, and aid in manageability. Some conditioners contain lanolin to add luster and sheen to a coat.

Stain removers. If your cat has a problem with excess tearing, a stain remover helps to eliminate tear stains under the eyes. Stain removers can also help remove urine and feces stains.

First, Clip Your Cat's Claws

If your cat's claws need clipping, begin the grooming session by clipping them. Your cat will need her toenails trimmed about every two to three weeks. This not only saves wear and tear on your furniture but also reduces the risk of your cat injuring you, your family, and your other pets. Having your cat knead in your lap is certainly a lot more comfortable if her nails are trimmed.

Before each show, your cat's nails will have to be trimmed. All associations require that the claws on all four feet be clipped prior to

Always clip your cat's nails before the grooming session.

benching, and failure to do so may be cause for disqualification. This is to protect the judges from injury while handling your cat. Clipping can also save you from having racing stripes on your arms.

Use either nail clippers designed for cats (available at any pet supply store) or heavy duty human nail clippers. With the cat held in your lap facing away from you, hold one paw and gently apply pressure on the paw to make the claws extend. Clip off the white part of the nail, being careful not to cut into the pink "quick." The quick is rich with nerve endings and hurts badly if cut. Think of that pain in terms of having a wood sliver rammed under your fingernail. Don't cut the white part of the nail any closer than a tenth of an inch from the quick. Just one experience with the "cruelest cut of all" and your cat will not react well to

Breeds with long, fine hair, like the Persian, will develop mats if their coats are not combed correctly.

having her nails clipped from then on. If you've never trimmed a cat's nails, you may want to ask your vet to show you how.

If your cat reacts badly to having her nails cut, enlist the help of a partner to get the job done, or catch the cat just after she has awakened from her afternoon nap and is sleepy. Be gentle and kind, and your cat will learn to accept nail trimming as just another of those incomprehensible things that humans do.

How to Comb or Brush a Show Cat

Pick a spot such as the bathroom, back porch, or other enclosed area to make cleanup easier if the fur flies. Before taking the cat to the grooming area, have all the grooming supplies ready and in place. That way you won't have to run off to find something and come back to find Fluffy hiding under the bed or chewing up the cotton swabs. Keeping all the grooming supplies in a caddy is a convenient way to keep them together and make transportation easy.

Run your hands over the cat's body, feeling for any swellings, lumps, growths, or abscesses. Check for tenderness, thin or bald spots, flea dirt, excessive skin flaking, and fur mats. Be sure to run your fingers over your cat's vaccination injection sites (usually between the shoulder blades or on the flanks)

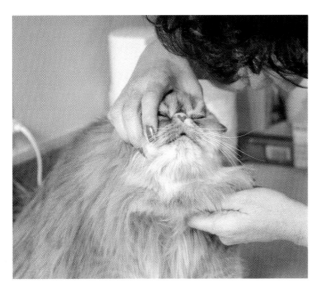

to detect possible injection site tumors called fibrosarcomas. Feel the tail gently for lumps, and the belly too, if your cat will hold still for it. Some cats react negatively when you touch their tummies and may try to scratch or to escape.

If the cat tries to run away or behaves aggressively while you are grooming her, limit the grooming session to a few minutes and slowly work up to longer sessions. Maybe you're being too rough. As you comb, watch your cat's body language. If she flattens her ears and lashes her tail, she's becoming angry. Take a break and return later when your cat has calmed down. Save the procedures your cat dislikes—such as nail clipping or bathing—for another time, so she doesn't associate her general grooming with these unpleasant activities.

Grooming the Longhair

After you have examined your cat, comb her fur thoroughly and gently in the direction of the lay of the fur, using a metal comb. Begin with the head and the back because your cat will probably enjoy being groomed in these areas. Work up to the more sensitive areas such as the sides, hindquarters, and belly. To groom the belly, lift your cat's front legs with one hand until the cat is standing on her rear legs, and comb

the belly and underarms with the other hand. Comb gently because these areas are sensitive, and talk softly to your cat. Many cats enjoy combing. Mother cats groom their kittens, and because your cat sees you as a surrogate parent, she ought to tolerate grooming without too much protest.

Make sure you comb all the way down to the skin. You can miss mats if you only comb the top layers. Be gentle, however, and don't push down hard on the comb. During this first comb through you are removing dead hair and looking for mats. These dense clumps of tangled hair often develop under the chin, behind the ears, under the arms, and on the belly and britches. They can be a serious health concern. Mats form next to the skin, causing pain and damage if the mat is not combed out or clipped promptly. The pain can be extreme, and nothing makes cats hate grooming faster than having their

Some Persian exhibitors put a ruff protector around their cat's neck before the show to protect the ruff's grooming.

101

hair pulled as knots are combed out. Mats can also become comfortable homes for fleas and other parasites.

If during this first gentle combing you notice mats in your cat's fur, put a bit of cornstarch on the mat and then gently work the mat free with the tip of the comb or with a mat-breaker tool. Hold the hair clump against the cat's body with your other hand while you work on the mat so you won't pull painfully on your cat's skin. If the mat is particularly stubborn, try sliding the comb in between the skin and the mat and snipping the mat on the side of the comb away from the skin. Use your blunt-tip scissors or a groomer's thinning shears, but be careful. A cat's skin is delicate, and it's easy to cut it accidentally, particularly if the cat wiggles at just the wrong moment. It only takes a painful snip or two for your cat to shoot under the bed when the cat comb comes out.

Make sure you remove all mats as soon as they appear. If your long-haired cat becomes badly matted, you may have to shave her coat. This will interrupt her show career until her hair grows out, and this takes time. Let a professional groomer or veterinarian handle severe matting problems.

If you suspect your cat has a problem with fleas, run the flea comb through her fur, particularly on the head, the base of the tail, and the underbelly. First set the cat on a light-colored towel so you can see any fleas or debris. If you do see

them, consult your vet for a course of treatment right away. Do not assume the problem can be solved with flea collars, especially on a longhaired cat. Collars can chafe and leave marks that can cost you points in the show ring.

After you have finished the initial exploratory combing and you have removed any mats and flea dirt, comb your cat again. This time, however, you should comb against the lie. This technique is known as backcombing. Use short strokes and deft flicks of the wrist to lift the hair away from the body and back away from the natural lie of the coat. Begin at the base of the tail and work up the back, and then down the sides. Then run the comb through the coat once more with the lie. End by holding the tail's tip and gently combing down the tail's length to fluff it like a bottle brush. Finally, comb the ruff forward to frame the face.

Many exhibitors end by powdering their cats with a powder formulated with cornstarch or another product specifically designed for cat coats. This helps separate the hairs, absorbs oils, and enhances the show look. Be careful with these, however. Some associations disqualify cats who have been excessively powdered. Comb all the powder out of the coat before taking your cat to the ring. It should go without saying, which is why it needs to be said, that colored chalk, tints, color rinses, and other cosmetics are also cause for disqualification.

Grooming the Shorthair

Hair density can vary greatly from breed to breed. Some breeds such as the Siamese, Oriental Shorthair, Bombay, Ocicat, and Burmese, have single-density, short, close lying coats that don't require much more than a gentle combing with a fine-toothed metal comb or rubber curry brush and a rub with a chamois. Other breeds, such as the Exotic Shorthair, British Shorthair, Chartreux, Manx, Russian Blue, and Scottish Fold, have dense, plush coats that stand away from the body. These breeds require more extensive combing to remove dead hair from the coat and to make the coat stand up and be noticed.

After examining the cat, comb your cat's fur with a fine-toothed metal comb. This applies to both single- and double-coated short-haired breeds. A double-coated breed is one in which the awn hairs (the intermediate layer of hairs in a cat's coat) are as long as the guard hairs (the outer layer of hairs). The down hairs are the shortest hairs in the coat.

The fine-toothed metal comb removes dead and loose hairs, catches fleas and flea dirt, and doesn't damage the cat's fur. Start grooming at the cat's head and work down to the tail, combing with the lie of the fur. Comb under the chin, on the neck, under the arms, behind the ears, under the belly, and around the hindquarters. Use the backcombing technique (see Grooming the Longhair on page 101) for breeds with dense coats. If you wish, you can finish the grooming session by going over the coat with a soft bristle brush or rubber curry brush. Finally, rub a chamois cloth over the coat to bring out the shine and to remove any final loose hairs.

Hairball Prevention

Once a week after grooming, treat your kitty to a dose of a petrolatum product such as Kittymalt or Petromalt to help prevent hairballs. To administer, smear a dab onto your finger and let your cat lick it off. Use such products only as directed. Too much can hinder the absorption of fat-soluble vitamins.

Bathing Your Cat

To keep your show cat looking her best, bathing is a necessity before each show. In addition if your cat has chronic problems with parasites or skin allergies, or does not properly attend to her grooming, regular bathing certainly benefits her health. Longhaired cats also have trouble keeping clean after a trip to the litter box.

Stud tail, an accumulation of waxy debris on the base of the tail caused by hyperactive sebaceous glands, is fairly common, particularly in unneutered male cats. Regular bathing will reduce these secretions and prevent the hair loss, irritation, and inflammation that can accompany this condition.

Routine cat bathing may benefit your health as well. Recent studies have shown that regular bathing of cats can remove a good percentage of the allergenic protein called Fel d1. This substance, secreted via saliva and sebaceous glands, triggers allergic reactions in humans.

You can bathe your cat in the kitchen sink or the bathtub. Many veterinarians recommend using a kitchen sink equipped with a spray hose attachment because you have more control over the cat when you're standing up. You can buy a rubber spray hose attachment for a few dollars at a bath supply store or large discount store. If your sink is too small or your cat too big, use the tub. Whatever you choose, be sure you can close off the area. Chasing a

wet, scared, soapy cat over the sofa and under the bed isn't much fun.

Before bathing your cat, trim her nails. Clean her ears, and plug them with a few cotton balls to prevent water and soap from getting into the cat's ear canals and possibly causing infection. You should also put a drop or two of mineral oil in each eye to protect them.

Before bathing the cat, comb her thoroughly. This is important for longhaired cats because bathing can set mats in the hair. As the coat dries, the mats tighten against the skin so they are impossible to remove. They must be cut out with scissors at that point.

Assemble all the needed supplies before you begin. You can use a flea-control shampoo (if necessary), a quality cat shampoo, or a gentle, protein-enriched shampoo designed for humans. Baby shampoo is fine. Don't use ordinary dish soap, which can dry out the cat's skin, and never use flea shampoo designed for dogs. The concentration of insecticide in dog shampoo can be harmful or even fatal to cats.

Mix the shampoo half and half with warm water in a plastic squeeze bottle with a closable valve top. Diluting the shampoo makes working it into the coat easier, and creates fewer suds so it's easier to rinse out completely. Do not dilute flea shampoo, however.

If you're using the sink, attach the spray nozzle and get the water to the proper temperature before fetching your cat. Keep the water near

A spray attachment makes rinsing your cat much easier.

the cat's normal body temperature of 101.4°F. Test the water on your arm. If it feels too hot for you, it will likely be too hot for your cat as well.

If you're bathing your cat in the tub, equip the faucet with a spray attachment. If the spray attachment won't fit your tub's faucet, put two rectangular basins inside the tub and fill them with water, one for wetting the cat, the second for rinsing. Run the bath water before you put the cat in. A cat's hearing is four times as good as ours and the sound of the water alarms cats. Dip your elbow into the water to make sure it's not too hot. Continue monitoring the water temperature throughout the bath.

Put your cat into the sink or tub with her back facing you so she won't scratch you if she strikes out or struggles. Hold her in place by applying gentle pressure to her shoulders. If she becomes uncontrollable, grip her by the nape of the neck and push down, being careful not to push her head under water, which will cause panic. Gripping the nape of the neck makes the cat freeze. Mother cats carry their young in this fashion. Never lift a full-grown cat by the nape. That can cause serious injury.

If your cat struggles, remain calm. Never yell at or strike her. That will frighten her further. A panicked cat can seriously injure you. Talk soothingly; your cat needs reassurance.

Use the nozzle to wet your cat's coat thoroughly. Don't wet above the neck line, but if she has fleas, wet and shampoo the neck area first to keep the fleas from escaping up the neck onto the head. Hold the spray attachment close to the cat's body. This scares the cat less than holding it farther away. Never spray the head, face, or ears, and never dunk a cat's head under water.

When your cat is completely wet, apply shampoo with the squeeze bottle. Work it well into the coat. Don't neglect the legs, feet, and tail, but be careful not to bend the tail tip as this can cause damage. Clean the hindquarters and the anal and genital areas, too, but be gentle. A soft washcloth is good for these areas.

After soaping your cat, rinse her well using the spray attachment. It's vital to get all the soap out of the fur because your cat grooms after her bath and ingests any remaining soap. Continue rinsing until the fur has lost the slick, soapy feel and the rinse water runs off clear with no foaming action.

Some owners finish off their cat's bath with hair rinse. This removes tangles and leaves the coat smooth. Others prefer a vinegar rinse because this helps remove any remaining shampoo. If you'd like to use a vinegar rinse, dilute a tablespoon of white vinegar in a quart of warm water and pour the rinse on your cat's fur. Make sure you keep the solution away from your cat's face. Massage the rinse into the coat, then rinse the coat with warm water.

After rinsing your cat thoroughly, run your hands down her body to remove excess water. Wrap her in a terry towel with just her head showing. Because you can't safely wash your cat's face while bathing, now's the time to use a warm, damp terry cloth washcloth to clean head, face, and chin. Be sure not to use anything that might scratch her eyes—paper towels, for example. Avoid getting soap in the eyes. If your cat struggles, stop washing until she calms down. Her struggles could cause you to poke her eyes. After washing her face, remember to remove the cotton plugs from her ears.

Exchange the towel for a fresh one and dry your cat well. Pat, don't rub, the fur. Rubbing creates tangles in longhaired cats. Change to a third towel if necessary. When the coat is toweled, it's time to dry your cat's fur.

Before blow drying, blot your cat as dry as possible with a towel.

Drying Your Cat

After bathing your shorthaired cat and using a towel to dry her, you can allow her coat to further air dry. When you've toweled her coat as dry as possible, leave her in an enclosed area to sulk and to groom herself. Don't let her into drafty areas until she is completely dry. Chilling is good for white wine, not felines. Most cats will groom continuously until they are dry.

Longhaired breeds will look much better and their fur will be smoother and fluffier if you blow dry it. This is particularly true of breeds such as the Persian. Indeed, blow-drying is essential for longhaired show cats.

The noise and sensation of the dryer frighten most cats, so begin training your cat early to tolerate the drier. Bring your cat into the bathroom while blow-drying your hair to show her that the dryer isn't dangerous. Cats learn by example. If you do not use a drier on your hair, set one on at the lowest speed while you are fixing her dinner.

When blow-drying your cat, use the drier on the lowest heat and lowest air speed settings. Avoid blowing air directly into your cat's face or ears. Test the dryer on your arm to make sure the air is not too hot.

Some cat owners use their cat carriers to begin the drying process, thereby avoiding the necessity of holding the cat and the drier at the same time. Nevertheless, you will need a drier stand, which you can buy from a pet-supply or grooming-supply outlet. Set up the dryer to blow into the wire door of the carrier, then leave your cat in carrier with the drier set on low for about 20 minutes. Never leave your cat unattended with the dryer turned on.

After 20 minutes take your cat from the carrier and finish drying her. The job will be easier if you have an assistant, but if you don't, set up the dryer in its stand and direct the air at the section of fur on which you are working. Start at the hindquarters and work your way up to the neck. Comb against the lie, pulling the hairs up and away from the body to separate and aerate the fur. Stand the cat up and dry her belly and underarms. This helps to prevent mats from forming and prevents the belly hair from drying in unsightly little corkscrews.

Using a cream rinse after bathing helps reduce static cling in the cat's fur. You can also use antistatic spray if you notice that flyaway look. These products are sold at pet supply or pet grooming stores. Be sure the label says "safe for cats."

Routine Ear and Eye Care

Grooming a show cat involves more than combing her. A show cat's ears and eyes need attention, too. Her eyes should be free of discharge and inflammation, and her inner eyelids (haws) should not protrude, as this can be a sign of seri-

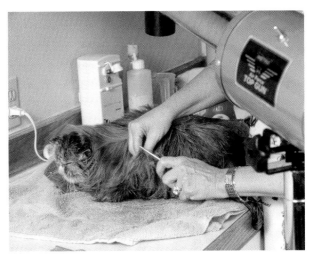

ous illness. The area around the eyes (particularly under the eyes), however, can accumulate dirt, dried tears, and sleep residue. Some breeds, such as the Persian, Exotic, and Himalayan, have a pronounced nose break and may have narrow or blocked tear ducts that can cause excess tearing. Tearing leaves ugly yellowish-brown spots on the facial fur. While you are grooming—or whenever your cat's face needs attention—wipe her eyes clean with a cotton ball moistened with warm (not hot) water. If the under-eye area develops stains, use a tear-stain remover available at pet supply stores. After your cat's face is clean, apply a slight amount of powder with a cotton swab to dry and aerate the fur beneath the eyes.

The ears of a normal, healthy cat should be clean and free of excessive waxy discharge. A healthy cat's ears shouldn't require much attention. If you notice dirt inside the flap,

A blow dryer with a hands-free stand makes drying your cat a lot easier. Always keep the dryer on the lowest heat setting to avoid burning your cat or damaging its fur.

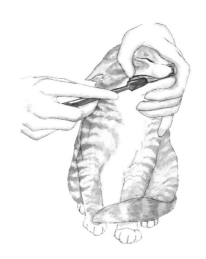

Bad teeth and inflamed gums (gingivitis) can make your cat's mouth so sore that it's hard for the cat to eat properly. Toothbrushing two or three times a week and dental check-ups can help prevent plaque and tartar buildup.

clean it with a cotton ball or swab moistened with a few drops of peroxide or olive oil. Don't poke the swab or any object into the ear canal, because you can damage the ear. If you see excessive dark waxy buildup, schedule an appointment with your veterinarian. Your cat may need treatment for ear mites.

Dental Care

A healthy cat's teeth are white and clean. The gums are firm and pink and closely attached to the teeth. A bright red line along the gum near the teeth is a sign of gingivitis—inflammation of the gums. Plaque deposits (a combination of bacteria, food particles, and saliva) harden onto tooth surfaces and become tartar. The plaque and tartar enlarge the pocket between the tooth and the gum. These pockets become ideal homes for bacteria that invade the gingival tissue, causing swelling and bleeding. Eventually, the teeth loosen and fall out. When gingivitis gets to this stage, the loose teeth must be removed and the remaining teeth cleaned in order for the inflammation to subside.

Spotting gingivitis is easy if you know what to look for. The classic signs are gum tenderness (your cat may cringe or flinch when you touch the side of her mouth), difficulty or pain when eating, drooling, and bad breath. The gums look red and inflamed, swollen, and sometimes have small whitish ulcers that bleed when touched. None of this will make a good impression upon the show judge. More important, your cat's health is your first concern. If you see these symptoms, schedule an appointment with your veterinarian. If untreated, gingivitis can also undermine your cat's health and affect your cat's kidneys, nervous system, heart, and liver.

Cats can get cavities, too. Cats develop tooth decay just under the gum line. The location makes it difficult to see the cavities. To prevent tooth loss and to control tartar and gingivitis, brush your cat's teeth regularly. Keeping your cat's teeth brushed extends the period between teeth cleanings and that cuts down on the expense and the risk to your cat, too, because cleaning a cat's teeth usually requires an anesthetic. Discuss your cat's tooth care with your veterinarian and get her recommendation about the proper products and toothbrushing frequency.

Many veterinarians carry dental products or can recommend the proper items, and many pet supply stores carry dental products as well. Buy a toothbrush designed for cats, or a soft child's size toothbrush. Buy one brush for each cat to prevent transmitting bacteria. Diluted hydrogen peroxide works well to clean the teeth and gums, and is inexpensive, or you can buy a toothpaste designed for cats. Don't use human toothpaste because the foam frightens cats and the swallowed paste may cause stomach upset. You can also buy feline stannous fluoride products to help strengthen the enamel and inhibit plaque formation.

Antibacterial gels to help reduce gum inflammation are also available.

Your cat can learn to tolerate having her teeth brushed if you exercise patience and care and if you brush her teeth regularly. Be careful not to hurt your cat because that will make her dread the process. When you begin, limit the time on each tooth to a few seconds and talk encouragingly to your cat the entire time. If possible, have someone hold your cat while you brush. Gently brush the tooth in a circular motion, and be careful on sensitive gums. You needn't brush the inside tooth surfaces usually because the cat's tongue cleans those. When you are finished brushing, praise your cat warmly and give her a treat.

Chapter 10

Show Hall Procedures

Remember, people will judge you by your actions, not your intentions. You may have a heart of gold—but so does a hard-boiled egg.

—Unknown

As you prepare for your first cat show, think of yourself as a football coach preparing a team for its first game of the season. Granted, showing cats is not a contact sport (unless you are trying to make your way to a judging ring in a crowded show hall), but in cat shows, as in football and real life, fortune smiles most beneficently on those who are most prepared when the whistle blows.

Checking In

Your cat has been bathed, groomed, and regroomed. You have trained him to tolerate the attentions of strangers. You have assembled, checked, rechecked, and packed all the supplies you will need to take to the show. You have allowed yourself a daydream or two about your cat's sterling performance in the ring. Now it is time to review your game plan. We begin with the check-in procedure.

Check-in serves two purposes. First, it allows exhibitors to obtain materials and information they will need on the day of the show. Second, it provides show officials with an idea of how many cats are going to be absent that day and how many cats will be transferred to classes other than the ones in which they were entered originally. (A cat must be transferred if its owner entered it in the wrong class for a show or if it is moving up in class because of wins it earned at shows it attended since the time it was entered in today's show.)

Your show flyer and/or confirmation notice will specify the check-in time, which usually begins two hours before judging starts and ends half an hour before the first cats are called to be judged. If you are a new exhibitor, you should arrive at the show hall to check in with plenty of time to spare. For example, if check-in is between 8:00 and 9:30 in the morning, be sure to arrive closer to 8:00 than to 9:30. Later, when you are a grizzled cat-show veteran with a rec room full of rosettes, you can breeze in at 9:20 A.M. with aplomb.

If the location of the check-in table is not immediately obvious to you when you arrive at the show, ask someone to point you in the right direction. When you reach the check-in table, show your entry confirmation to the first helpful looking person you see there (you did remember your entry confirmation, didn't you?). That helpful looking person, usually the entry clerk or one of his assistants, will give you a cage card to put on your cat's cage. Your cat's catalog number is printed on this card. You may also receive promotional information about special events at the show, a complimentary pencil or pen for marking catalogs, and other handouts.

If the price of a show catalog was not included in your entry fee, be sure to buy a catalog at the check-in table so you can have the thrill of seeing your and your cat's names in print and, more practically, so you can check to see that this information has been recorded accurately. (Although you checked the data on your entry confirmation to see that it was correct when you first received the confirmation, you should check the catalog anyway to see that all the name-rank-and-serial-number information has been printed correctly. If you find any errors at this point, ask someone to direct you to the master clerk and tell him about the mistake.)

You should also obtain a judging schedule so that you will know the appropriate rings and the appropriate times at which you will present your cat. The judging schedule is

printed in some catalogs; in others, the schedule is printed on separate sheets of paper inserted in each catalog.

After obtaining you cat's cage number, a show catalog, and a schedule, ask the entry clerk for directions to the spot in the show hall where your cat will be benched (i.e., caged) when it is not being judged. Also ask where litter and litter pans are stored and where to get fresh water for your cat.

If you arrive at the show hall after check-in has closed, you will have to tell the ring clerk at each ring in which your cat is scheduled to compete that your cat is indeed present and that its name should be removed from the absentee list. (The ring clerk is usually the person sitting at the judging table, not the person standing behind the table.

When you get to the show, check in right away.

That person is the judge, and she is not concerned at this point whether your cat is in the show hall or not.) The best way to inform ring clerks that your cat is present is to write your cat's catalog number followed by the words "is present" on as many slips of paper as there are rings in which your cat is scheduled to be judged that day. Then give one of those slips of paper to the ring clerk at each ring in which your cat is scheduled to be judged.

Some two-day shows require that you check in the second morning of the show also. This second check-in usually consists of nothing more than telling someone at the check-in table that cat number such-and-such (your cat) is present. Again, if a second check-in is required and you miss it, you will have to inform each ring clerk that your cat is present.

Setting Up

When cats are not being judged, they are housed in rectangular, wire cages. These cages, which have hinged tops but no bottoms, rest on individual wood-and-particle-board bottoms that, in turn, rest on trestles about 3 feet (.9 m) high. There are many rows of cages set up for a show—how many depends on the number of cats entered—and there are usually a dozen or so cages in each row.

Cleaning Your Cat's Cage

Cat cages are light enough to lift off their bottoms, and most exhibitors do so in order to set up and to clean a cage before putting a cat in it. Spraying a cage and a cage bottom with disinfectant and wiping it off carefully before decorating that cage and placing a cat in it will help to prevent the spread of any long-lived disease from a cage's occupants at a previous show to its occupants at the present one.

Decorating Your Cat's Cage

While the cage is on the floor, you can fit a rug or towels over the cage bottom. After returning the cage to its trestle-supported bottom, swing the top of the cage back and install the cage curtains on the inside of the cage, securing them in place with clips, snaps, or clothespins. Fill a litter pan with an inch or so of litter and place the pan at one end of the cage, then arrange any other furniture—a bed, cat toys, and so on—that you have brought to the show. After you have swung the cage top back into place, make sure it is fastened securely in case something in this strange new world frightens your cat. Many exhibitors put a covering of some sort over the top of the cage. Finally, put your cat into the cage and close the cage door securely.

Most show cages are roughly 22 inches (56 cm) tall, 22 inches (56 cm) wide, and 44 inches (112 cm) long, with a hinged, moveable divider in the center that can be used to separate each cage into two smaller cages. The "cage" to which exhibitors are assigned, therefore, is actually one half of a double cage. Thus, most exhibitors will be sharing a duplex that is 22 inches (56 cm) high, wide, and tall with someone else at the show. If that person already has set up his half of the double cage, disinfecting your side of the cage and installing your rug and cage curtains will require a little more manual dexterity than if you had the entire cage to yourself. You should be careful not to disturb your neighbor's half of the cage or your neighbor's cat when you are spraying and decorating your half. Obviously you should not swing the cage top back to install your curtains if there is already a cat in the other half of the cage. Imagine your dismay at seeing the cat in the adjoining half of the cage go sailing over the side and racing for the door.

Cats at shows may want to play, but diseases can be spread through casual contact. Keep your kitty out of harm's way by making sure other cats can't reach through.

Some exhibitors feed their cats after the cats have finished sniffing about their cages. Other exhibitors wait until later in the day to feed. (If you are showing a breed in which svelte is beautiful, you do not want to overfeed your cat at the show. A cat cannot look svelte if its stomach pooches out as if the cat had just swallowed the canary.) Whether you feed your cat at the show or not, you should offer him water after he is settled in his cage. Some exhibitors

Some fanciers go all out to make their cat's cage attractive and comfortable.

Cats that have never been shown before will probably find all the noise and confusion frightening. Spend some time reassuring your cat and provide enough bedding and cage coverings so the cat can feel secure.

leave a water bowl in the cage all day. Others offer their cats a drink periodically throughout the day. The choice is yours. In making that choice remember that a cat cannot spill what he cannot get his paws on.

Do not go running off to spy on your competition as soon as you have put your cat in his cage. Spend a few minutes talking to him soothingly (a cat show is one of the few places where you can talk to a cat in public without calling attention to yourself). After all, you brought your cat to this strange place; you should let him know that you will see him home safely.

The Judging Schedule

Now that your cat has been installed in his cage, consult the judging schedule to see how often and at what times he will be judged that day. If you have arrived at the

show hall early during the check-in period, there should be plenty of time left to do this before the start of judging. The judging schedule lists the order in which classes will be called to the various rings. The rings are listed across the top of the page and the order of classes for each ring is listed underneath each ring. Your entry confirmation notice will tell you (in case you have forgotten) the class in which your cat or kitten is entered. Begin with the first ring and look down the schedule of classes for that ring to find the class in which your cat is entered. Circle your cat's class then repeat this procedure for each ring, but don't relax altogether and tune out the public address system entirely. (Cats are called to the judging rings via the public address system.) Judging schedules are subject to change, and if you fail to make a class because you didn't hear the announcement about a change in schedule, it's your loss.

Now that you know where you have to go, the next question is: When do you have to be there? This is not as challenging as solving differential equations, but you should pay attention to ring calls throughout the day to see how close your cat is to being due in a ring.

For example, if your cat is going to be judged in rings 3, 5, 9, and 10 and you hear such-and-such a breed (or class) being called to ring 5, look to see how far ahead of your cat's class that just-called breed or class is. When the breed (or class) immediately preceding your cat's is called, you can begin any last-minute grooming and say any last-minute prayers before your cat's class is called and you haul him off to battle.

To the Ring We Go

Different folks use different strokes to get a cat from its benching cage to the judging ring. Some exhibitors charge down even the most crowded aisles; others mince along. The best approach is to move confidently and purposefully as though you were making your way across a hotel lobby to a waiting limousine. In addition be sure to have a secure grip on your cat. Hold your forearm palm up, arm parallel to the ground. Position your cat so that its front and rear legs straddle your forearm. Cup the cat's chest in your palm, securing one front leg between your thumb and forefinger, and the other front leg between your ring and little fingers. Should your cat become startled on the way to the ring, stop for a moment, bring your forearm close to your body, and use your free hand (and your voice) to comfort your cat.

Invariably someone and his family will ask if they can pet your cat. Just say no, politely, and explain that you are on your way to the judging ring and that they are all welcome to come and watch your cat being judged. You will make a good impression if you arrive at the ring with an entourage. If you get a

request for petting privileges on your way back from the ring, just say no, smile, and explain that your cat does not allow petting on the first date.

Upon arriving at the judging ring, look for a cage with your cat's number on top and place your cat in that cage. Fasten the cage door securely, then take a seat in the gallery.

You'll know which cage to put your cat into because it will be marked with your cat's number.

As you carry your cat to the judging ring, stay alert and call out "Cat through!" to alert the people around you. You don't want to lose your kitty in the crowd.

Don't touch that kitty! It is best not to touch the cats you meet in the show hall. Hand-to-hand contact can spread feline disease.

Like most eagerly awaited events in life, a cat's interval on the judging table is brief and somewhat anticlimactic, about 90 seconds on the average. During that time, judges compare a cat to the standard for its breed (see The Judging Schedule, page 114). After handling all the entries in a class or division, judges hang ribbons whose text and colors proclaim the placement of each ribbon winning contestant in the group (see Scoring Procedures, page 64). The ring clerk then dismisses the class by saying, "These cats can go back," or by simply turning down the numbers on the tops of cats' cages. After your cat has been dismissed, tell him what a good job he did as you return him to his benching cage, then check your judging schedule to see when he is going to be judged again.

Decamping

Most show committees expect exhibitors to remain in the show hall with their cats on display in their benching cages until the advertised closing time for the show. If that time arrives and your cat is finished being judged for the day—and the show in which you are entered is a one-day show—you may pack up your belongings and go home. If you have entered a two-day show, there is no need to take down your cage curtains and rug after the first day's competition. You will need them again tomorrow. Indeed, you may leave anything you want, except your cat, of course, in the show hall overnight. To be safe, however, do not leave anything valuable.

A Few Final Thoughts

Mark Twain, who knew something about human nature and cats, once observed that it is difference of opinion that makes horse races. The same applies to cat shows. Judges spend one to two minutes evaluating each cat. They often make more than two hundred of these rapid-fire assessments per show. For this expertise judges receive from 35 cents to a dollar for every cat they judge. Exhibitors who disagree with judges' decisions sometimes complain that a judge's opinion is not even worth that.

It is hard to bring your beloved show cat to the show ring and watch her lose to a cat that is—in your opinion—of lesser merit. Taking rejection in any form is hard, and it's doubly hard when the rejection is aimed at your beloved feline who you think is the smartest, most beautiful, and best behaved example of the breed. How could anyone look into those trusting, brilliant eyes and think anything else? It hurts your feelings and crushes your hopes of coming home with your opinion of your cat validated by professional judges. It's natural to want to express you frustration, disagreement, and anger—but don't. At least, don't do it in front of the judges and other exhibitors. Later, at home, you can voice your woes to your understanding spouse and supportive friends—both human and feline. Expressing your disagreement to the judge will not make him change his mind about his decision. Declaring your resentment of the winner to the other exhibitors will only make you look like a sore loser. Even if your cat doesn't bring home a ribbon, your cat is still your loyal companion and always will be "best of breed" in your household. Remember that the judges' opinions are just that—opinions. Judges are human and they can make mistakes. Try again. The next judge may have another view.

Remember also that winning isn't the only reason to attend a cat show. Of course you'd like to come home with a rosette. Who wouldn't?

But if the factor that determines whether you have an enjoyable weekend or a miserable one is winning that rosette, you're losing sight of the bigger picture. The cat fancy was developed to bring together fanciers of cats—people who share your love of their myriad conformations, patterns, and colors, your fascination with their mystery and

After putting your cat in the proper cage, sit in the gallery so you can watch your cat being judged.

Cats that are calm, confident, and playful impress the judges.

elegance, and your enjoyment of their unique personalities. Treat all cats and the people who love them with courtesy and respect—and be polite to the folks who have dropped by to watch the action, too. Remember that through our actions the cat fancy is judged, and we should all work to earn rosettes in courtesy, consideration, and compassion.

If you go to the show to have fun, as well as to win, you will have enjoyed a unique experience, made friends, developed a better understanding of cats and the cat fancy and, hopefully, strengthened the bond between you and your favorite feline. That, in the end, is what's important.

Glossary

AACE The American Association of Cat Enthusiasts.

ACA The American Cat Association.

ACFA The American Cat Fanciers Association.

Agouti Hairs that are "ticked" with alternating bands of light and dark color, ending with a dark tip.

Allbreed Refers to a judge who is qualified to judge all of the cat breeds.

Alter A cat that has been spayed or neutered.

AOC Any other color.

AOV Any other variety; applies to any registered cat or kitten whose ancestry entitles it to championship competition but that does not conform to the show standard.

Awn A secondary hair type coarser than the down hairs; these hairs form an insulating layer.

Balance A cat's physical and temperamental balance. When the cat's parts are not in proper proportion, the cat is said to be out of balance.

Benching The area of the show hall where exhibitors display their cats.

Best in Show An award given to the cat judged to be the finest example for the entire cat show.

Best of Breed An award given to the cat judged to be the finest example of the breed in that show ring. A Best of Breed is chosen for each ring.

Bicolor A cat that is white and one other color.

Blaze A marking on the center of the forehead between the eyes; often runs down the nose as well.

Bloodline A group of cats related by ancestry or pedigree.

Blue A soft gray coat color.

Bracelet A ringed marking in the tabby pattern that encircles the legs.

CAUTION — KEEP OUT
BEWARE OF CATS
VIOLATORS WILL BE EATEN
SURVIVORS WILL BE PROSECUTED

Spectators lean forward in anticipation as the judge makes her decision.

Break An indentation of the nose at about eye level or between the eyes.

Breeches Longer hair on the back of the upper hind legs.

Brindle A scattering of the "wrong" colored hairs in another color.

Calico A cat with patches of black, red, and white.

Cameo A cat that possesses a red coat with white roots. Also called shaded or smoke.

Carrier A cat carrying an unexpressed recessive gene that is able to pass that gene on to its offspring. Also can mean a container used to transport cats.

Cat show An event, usually held on the weekend, where cats are shown and judged.

Cat fancy The group of people, associations, clubs, and registries involved in the showing and breeding of cats.

Cattery A room or area in the breeder's house, or building on the breeder's property, where cats are housed and bred.

CCA Canadian Cat Association.

CFA The Cat Fanciers' Association.

CFF The Cat Fanciers' Federation.

Champion A cat that has achieved championship status in an association.

Chinchilla A coat type where the white hairs are barely tipped with black.

Chocolate A rich medium brown coat color.

Cinnamon A reddish brown color.

Closing date The date the entry clerk must have your entry for your cat to be eligible for competition in the show.

Cobby A broad, round body type, like that of the Persian and Exotic Shorthair.

Conformation The physical type of the cat, which includes coat length, color, bone structure, facial type, and many other factors.

Crossbreeding The allowable mating of two pedigree varieties.

Dam Mother of a kitten or litter.

Declawed Said of a cat that has had its claws surgically removed. Some associations don't allow declawed cats to be shown.

Dilute A soft, pale version of a dominant color.

Dilute calico A cat with patches of blue, cream, and white.

Disqualification Elimination from cat show competition because of a serious fault.

Dome Rounded forehead of a cat.

Domestic A non-pedigreed cat.

Dominant Said of a genetic trait that masks the effects of recessive genes.

Double coat A coat possessing a thick layer of awn and down hairs.

Down A secondary hair type that is soft and slightly wavy; much shorter than guard hairs.

Entire Describing a cat that has not been spayed or neutered.

Exhibitor A fancier who has entered a cat into competition.

Fault A flaw in the color, coat, or conformation of a cat, causing a loss of awarded points.

Fawn A warm pink or buff color.

Felis catus The species of domestic cat.

Feral Said of a domesticated animal that has reverted to the wild or that has been born in the wild.

Final The awarding of the rosettes to the top cats in each category.

Foreign A body type of oriental appearance, as in the Siamese; sometimes called Oriental.

Furnishings Refers to the hair inside the ears.

GCCF Governing Council of the Cat Fancy; the main cat registry in Britain.

Genes Units of heredity that control growth, development, and function of organisms.

Genetics The study of heredity.

Genotype The genetic composition of a cat, whether or not expressed in the physical appearance.

Ghost markings Faint tabby markings seen in some solid colored cats; particularly noticeable in young cats.

Grand Champion A cat that has qualified for this award within a particular association.

Ground color The lighter color in between the darker color in the tabby patterns.

Guard hairs The longest of the three hair types; they form the coat's outer layer.

Harlequin A mostly white cat with patches of color, usually on the extremities.

Himalayan pattern Pattern where the color is concentrated at the extremities of the body; also called the Siamese pattern.

Hock The ankle of the cat's hind leg.

Household pet (HHP) A random bred cat, or a purebred cat that is not registered or cannot compete with members of its breed. These cats compete in a special category called the Household Pet or HHP category.

Hybrid The offspring of two different breeds.

Jowls Cheek folds that are prominent in unneutered male cats.

Judging cage Individual cages in the show ring used to hold the cats awaiting judging.

Judging schedule Schedule that sets the order in which each judge will see the day's categories.

Kink A bend or bump in the tail; usually grounds for disqualification in show cats.

Laces White fur that extends from the paws up the back of the leg.

Lavender A pale pinkish gray shade; also called lilac.

Litter A family of kittens. Can also mean matter used as toilet material.

Locket A solid white spot.

Mask A darker area on the face, including the nose, whisker pads, chin, and around eyes.

Master clerk The person who compiles the information from the judging rings into one master catalog.

Mittens White areas restricted to the feet.

Mutation A change or "mistake" in a gene that results in a change in hereditary characteristics between two generations.

Muzzle The part of the head that includes the nose, whisker pads, chin, mouth, jaws, and cheeks.

Muzzle break An indentation where the muzzle attaches to the skull; also called a whisker break or whisker pinch.

Necklace Darker markings encircling the neck.

New breed A breed of cat that is in the process of being developed and has not achieved championship status.

Nose leather Area of colored skin on nose, not covered by fur.

Odd eyes or odd eyed Refers to a cat whose eyes are of two different colors; for example, one blue and one copper eye.

Oriental A long, slender body type, as in the Siamese; also called foreign.

Outcrossing The breeding of one registered breed to another, resulting in a registerable hybrid breed. Also refers to the breeds allowable in the background of a registered hybrid breed.

Papers Usually refers to a cat's pedigree or certificate of registration.

Particolor Having either two or more colors (depending upon the association), or having any color or pattern with white.

Pattern The color distribution on a cat's coat that forms a particular pattern, such as the striped tabby pattern.

Paw pads The furless padded areas under the feet.

Pedigreed cat A cat whose heritage is documented and registered.

Phenotype The outward appearance of a cat.

Plane Surface.

Points The extremities of a cat's body, head, ears, tail, and feet. Also can mean the points awarded in the show ring.

Polydactyl A cat that has extra toes; considered a show fault.

Polygenes Groups of genes that are small in effect individually, but that act together to produce greater bodily characteristics.

Premier An altered, registered purebred cat.

Pricked Refers to ears held erect.

Queen A breeding female cat.

Random bred A cat that is not bred intentionally and whose ancestry is not known.

Recessive A characteristic that is unable to express itself in the cat's physical appearance in the presence of the alternate dominant characteristic.

Recognition Official acceptance by one of the cat associations of a new breed or color.

Registration Initial recording of a cat's individual name and owner.

Ring clerk The person who keeps track of the entries being judged and records the judge's decisions.

Ring The area in which judging takes place.

Roman nose A nose with a bump.

Ruddy A reddish brick color used to describe Abyssinians and Somalis.

Sable A dark brown.

Scoring The system of keeping track of the number of points and awards each cat has attained. Each association has a separate system.

Seal Deep brown color. Most often refers to Siamese and other pointed cats.

Self-colored Solid colored.

Show cage One of the cages in the benching area where the entries are kept until it's time for them to be shown.

Sire Father of a kitten or litter.

Smoke A coat color that appears to be a solid color but that possesses white roots.

Standards The standards of perfection that outline the ideal conformation for each breed.

Status The award level for which a particular cat has qualified, such as grand champion.

Stop A change in the slope of the profile.

Stud A male cat used for breeding.

Stud book Records maintained by the cat registries that record cats' offspring.

Svelte Slender, firm, and trim.

TICA The International Cat Association.

Tipped A coat type that has colored ends to the hairs.

Tortie or tortoiseshell Combination of black and orange or their dilutes.

Tubular Cylindrical; having the form of a tube.

Type The cat's conformation.

UFO The United Feline Organization.

Undercoat The awn and down hairs.

Undercolor The color on the hair shaft closest to the skin.

Van pattern Bicolor in which the cat is mostly white with colored patches on the head and tail.

Wedge Used to describe a particular head type. A geometric shape with two principal planes meeting in a sharply acute angle.

Whippy Tail type seen in breeds such as the Sphynx, Oriental, and Siamese.

Whisker break An indentation where the muzzle attaches to the skull. Also called a whisker pinch or muzzle break.

Whole Said of a cat that has not been spayed or neutered.

Useful Addresses and Literature

American and Canadian Cat Associations

American Association of Cat
Enthusiasts (AACE)
P.O. Box 213
Pine Brook, NJ 07058
(973) 335-6717
www.aaceinc.org

American Cat Association (ACA)
8101 Katherine Avenue
Panorama City, CA 91402
(818) 781-5656
(818) 781-5340 Fax

American Cat Fanciers Association
(ACFA)
P.O. Box 203
Pt. Lookout, MO 65726
(417) 334-5430
www.acfacat.com

Canadian Cat Association (CCA)
220 Advance Blvd., Suite 101
Brampton, Ontario
Canada L6T 4J5
(905) 459-1481
www.cca-afc.com

Cat Fanciers' Association (CFA)
1805 Atlantic Avenue
P.O. Box 1005
Manasquan, NJ 08736
(732) 528-9797
www.cfa@cfainc.org

Cat Fanciers' Federation (CFF)
9509 Montgomery Road
Cincinnati, OH 45242
(937) 787-9009
(937) 787-4290 Fax
www.cffinc.org

National Cat Fanciers' Association
(NCFA)
20305 West Burt Road
Brant, Michigan 48614
(517) 585-3179

The International Cat Association
(TICA)
P.O. Box 2684
Harlingen, TX 78551
(956) 428-8046
www.tica.org

Traditional Cat Association, Inc.
(TCA)
18509 NE 279th Street
Battle Ground, WA 98604-9717
www.covesoft.com/tca/

United Feline Organization (UFO)
P.O. Box 3234
Olympia, WA 98509-3234
(360) 438-6903
members.aol.com/ufo1nw/ufoweb.
html

Miscellaneous Organizations and Agencies

American Humane Association
P.O. Box 1266
Denver, CO 80201
(303) 792-9900

American Society for the Prevention
of Cruelty to Animals (ASPCA)
424 East 92nd Street
New York, NY 10128
(212) 876-7700

Animal People (Nonprofit organization whose newsletter provides
information on animal charities)
P.O. Box 960
Clinton, WA 98236-0960

Best Friends Animal Sanctuary
Kanab, UT 84741
(801) 644-2001

Cornell Feline Health Center
New York State College of
Veterinary Medicine
Cornell University
Ithaca, NY 14853

The Delta Society
P.O. Box 1080
Renton, WA 98057
(206) 226-7357

Friends of Animals
P.O. Box 1244
Norwalk, CT 06856
(800) 631-2212
(For low-cost spay/neuter program
information)

Fund for Animals
200 West 57th Street
New York, NY 10019
(212) 246-2096

The Humane Society of the United
States (HSUS)
2100 L Street N.W.
Washington, DC 20037
(202) 452-1100

People for the Ethical Treatment
of Animals (PETA)
501 Front Street
Norfolk, VA 23510

Pets Are Wonderful Support
(PAWS)
P.O. Box 460489
San Francisco, CA 94146
(415) 241-1460
(Provides pet-related services for
people with AIDS)

Robert H. Winn Foundation for
Cat Health
1805 Atlantic Avenue
P.O. Box 1005
Manasquan, NJ 08736-1005
(Established by the CFA)

Cat Magazines

CATS
2 News Plaza
P.O. Box 1790
Peoria, IL 61656
(309) 682-6626

Cat Fancy
P.O. Box 6050
Mission Viejo, CA 92690
(714) 855-8822

Cat Fancier's Almanac
P.O. Box 1005
Manasquan, NJ 08736-0805
(908) 528-9797

Catnip (newsletter)
Tufts University School of
    Veterinary Medicine
P.O. Box 420014
Palm Coast, FL 32142-0014
(800) 829-0926

Cat World
10 Western Road
Shoreham-By-Sea
West Sussex, BN43 5WD
England

I Love Cats
950 3rd Avenue, 16th Floor
New York, NY 10022-2705
(212) 888-1855

Cat Watch
Cornell University College of
    Veterinary Medicine Newsletter
P.O. Box 420235
Palm Coast, FL 32142-0235
(800) 829-8893

Books

Collier, Marjorie McCann. *Siamese Cats.* Hauppauge, New York: Barron's Educational Series, Inc., 1992.

Davis, Karen Leigh. *The Exotic Shorthair Cat.* Hauppauge, New York: Barron's Educational Series, Inc., 1997.

___. *Fat Cat, Finicky Cat.* Hauppauge, New York: Barron's Educational Series, Inc., 1997.

___. *Somali Cats.* Hauppauge, New York: Barron's Educational Series, Inc., 1996.

___. *Turkish Angora Cats.* Hauppauge, New York: Barron's Educational Series, Inc., 1998.

Frye, Fredric. *First Aid for Your Cat.* Hauppauge, New York: Barron's Educational Series, Inc., 1987.

Helgren, J. Anne. *Abyssinian Cats.* Hauppauge, New York: Barron's Educational Series, Inc., 1995.

___. *Himalayan Cats.* Hauppauge, New York: Barron's Educational Series, Inc., 1996.

___. *Barron's Encyclopedia of Cat Breeds.* Hauppauge, New York: Barron's Educational Series, Inc., 1997.

Himsel Daly, Carol. *Caring for Your Sick Cat.* Hauppauge, New York: Barron's Educational Series, Inc., 1994.

___. *Maine Coon Cats.* Hauppauge, New York: Barron's Educational Series, Inc., 1994.

Lessmeier, Friedhelm. *The British Shorthair Cat.* Hauppauge, New York: Barron's Educational Series, Inc., 1997.

Maggitti, Phil. *Before You Buy That Kitten.* Hauppauge, New York: Barron's Educational Series, Inc., 1995.

___. *Birman Cats.* Hauppauge, New York: Barron's Educational Series, Inc., 1996.

___. *Guide to a Well-Behaved Cat.* Hauppauge, New York: Barron's Educational Series, Inc., 1993.

___. *Scottish Fold Cats.* Hauppauge, New York: Barron's Educational Series, Inc., 1993.

Müller, Ulrike. *The Cat.* Hauppauge, New York: Barron's Educational Series, Inc., 1997.

___. *Healthy Cat, Happy Cat.* Hauppauge, New York: Barron's Educational Series, Inc., 1995.

___. *Persian Cats.* Hauppauge, New York: Barron's Educational Series, Inc., 1990.

Pinney, Chris C. *Caring for Your Older Cat.* Hauppauge, New York: Barron's Educational Series, Inc., 1996.

Rice, Dan. *Bengal Cats.* Hauppauge, New York: Barron's Educational Series, Inc., 1995.

___. *The Complete Book of Cat Breeding.* Hauppauge, New York: Barron's Educational Series, Inc., 1996.

Vella, Carolyn, and John McGonagle. *Burmese Cats.* Hauppauge, New York: Barron's Educational Series, Inc., 1995.

Viner, Bradley. *The Cat Care Manual.* Hauppauge, New York: Barron's Educational Series, Inc., 1986.

Wright, Michal and Salley Walters, ed. *The Book of the Cat.* New York: Summit Books, 1980.

Index

The complexities of cat shows are explained clearly and completely by two veteran breeders and exhibitors in this *tour de force* of the cat fancy. Whether you are a spectator who wants to learn more about how cats are judged, a beginning cat fancier thinking about showing your cat, or an experienced exhibitor who would like to add to your store of feline facts, this book will take you step-by-step through the intricacies of the cat show world.